Stop the Merry-go-round

by
Don Mallough

BAKER BOOK HOUSE
Grand Rapids, Michigan
1964

PHOTOLITHOPRINTED BY CUSHING - MALLOY, INC.
ANN ARBOR, MICHIGAN, UNITED STATES OF AMERICA
1964

To the congregation of Faith Tabernacle, Tulsa, Oklahoma,

Whose love for the Word of God makes preaching easy.

Prologue

The sermons in this volume were forged on the anvil of a busy pastorate. The blueprint has called for Bible-centered truths to challenge and meet the needs of the average person. How well the artisan has followed through on that plan must be judged by the reader.

Many of these messages are appearing in print for the first time. Some, however, have been carried in past years by such magazines as *The Gospel Herald, Daily Blessings, The Sunday School Counselor, Pulpit* and *The Pentecostal Evangel*. Sincere thanks are expressed to the editors of these publications for kindly granting permission to put them in this more permanent form.

If the truths on these pages enrich and inspire the reader only a fraction of what they did for the author, when preparing and delivering them, then this book will have served its purpose.

Don Mallough

Tulsa, Oklahoma
October 1963

Contents

1. Stop the Merry-go-round! 11
2. A Second Funeral for Lazarus 15
3. The Life of One Dimension 20
4. What Did the Sheep Say? 25
5. Message from a Moslem Mosque 29
6. Remove the Blindfold! 33
7. The Afterglow 37
8. Hallowed Desert Sands 40
9. The Dejected Hero 45
10. The Commander-in-Chief 49
11. Deliberate Delay 53
12. Restrained Righteousness 57
13. The Underprivileged Failure 62
14. A Crusader, But 67
15. Subtle Slumber 71
16. When the Twin Missed Church 76
17. The Blunted Thorn 80
18. Marks of Maturity 85
19. Pickets at the Pearly Portals 90
20. The Haunting Lament 94

1

Stop the Merry-go-round

"Ye have compassed this mountain long enough: turn you northward." — Deuteronomy 2:3

While waiting for a train I saw a sight that was both amusing and revealing. Right near the depot was a small street carnival and from where I stood I could see the merry-go-round. There was the sound of the calliope mingled with laughter and the cries of delight that came from the children as they bounced up and down on the wooden horses.

One father put his four-year-old on the horse for his first ride. After overcoming the initial sense of fear, the boy grinned with glee as he circled, and the proud parent waved wildly and called to him as he passed. When the ride came to an end the father attempted to help him off the horse. The little fellow put up a violent protest. He screamed, cried, and clung tenaciously to the pole.

Finally, in great embarrassment, the father reached into his coin purse, bought another ticket, and the storm subsided. That ride, too, came to an end. Rather gently the father said, "Come now, Billy, we must go home." That did not appeal to the lad at all and he duplicated his original performance. If anything, he was more determined to stay on than ever.

Again the father's efforts were unavailing. He weakened and bought a third ticket. The whole experience was repeated several times and each time it became more humorous to the onlooker. After the eighth trip the boy was just as eager to ride, as adamant against dismounting, and put on as violent a demonstration as at the first. Finally the disgusted father said, "Billy, we're going home!" Then by sheer force he pulled him off the horse and dragged the screaming, kicking boy in the direction of his car.

That parent had to take drastic action and he might as well have done it the first time.

Riding the merry-go-round is a pleasant pastime for children — and for some adults. In the spiritual realm it is also a common practice of those who are childish and immature. There comes a time when we must dismount from the wooden horses and go on a real journey. Like an earthly parent, God, our heavenly Father, must take drastic action to put a stop to our senseless circling. Often He must do so over our protests because we greatly delight in playing games and would rather pretend to be traveling than to journey toward our destination.

God took such action centuries ago for His people the Israelites. He did so by giving them a stiff command. They had been traveling in circles and He veritably said to them, "Stop the merry-go-round!" Those were not His exact words but that is the essence of His message when He said, "Ye have circled this mountain long enough." If we but incline our ears to hear the voice of God we will hear the same message today.

The sin of Israel was that of meandering. They took forty years to traverse an area they could have covered in forty days. They were constantly moving but gaining no ground. They played at traveling by merely going in circles.

The Israelites had completely lost sight of their goal. They were glad to have left Egypt, with all of its evils and discomforts, but had forgotten God's purpose in bringing them out. They had started with the objective of reaching the promised land but had long since forgotten about that. They had ceased being travelers and had become tramps. They knew only the mechanics of packing and moving. They had no vision as to where they were going.

God reminded them that they were only marking time. They were treading too long in the same place and traversing the same territory. Because we tend to do as they did we too need a jarring rebuke and a stirring to action. To those of us who are in a rut He says, "Ye have circled this mountain long enough." In a jolting exclamation, in modern parlance, He says, "Stop the merry-go-round!"

We are very prone to go in the circle of tradition. We do things, even in worship, because we have done them always. Eventually those traditions become stronger than convictions which are based upon, "Thus saith the Lord." It is very easy to become a slave to the methods of the past which merely keep us going in circles. We follow in the rut of past custom and think we are progressing when we are actually beating over the same trails.

Some families have a long-established custom whereby the head of the household reads Dickens' *A Christmas Carol* every Christmas eve. The younger generation in such a family assumes such reading is essential to Christmas. There is nothing wrong with such a practice but tradition lays greater emphasis upon that one piece of literature than it rightly deserves. To some it is more important than the gospel account of Christmas. There comes a time to leave the mount of tradition and follow the leadings of the Lord. Even worse are the traditions that are at cross points with the revealed will of God. Jesus strongly rebuked the Pharisees by saying, "Ye reject the commandment of God, that ye may keep your own tradition" (Mark 7:9).

It is very easy to travel in the circle of complacency. How readily we become smug, satisfied and content. God has led us out of the Egypt of sin and we find wilderness living better than the old life. That it falls far short of the Canaan life that was promised to us we do not consider. We show little concern for our spiritual betterment and none for the condition of the lost ones about us. Our attitude says, "I am enjoying myself and I shall not be moved."

Many of us have settled into the groove of seeking self-comfort primarily. It is most revealing to take an inventory of what we want most and what we would spend hard-earned money to obtain. The creature comforts are high on the list; good food, fine clothes, a reclining chair in which to relax, a comfortable mattress on the bed or a vibrator to lull us to sleep. Fleshly comfort and ease take first place on our want list. The body is pampered and made to be king instead of servant, as in the Scriptural teachings. Feelings have a louder voice than the Lord. God says, "Not forsaking the assembling of ourselves together . . . but exhorting one another, and so much the more as ye see the day approaching" (Hebrews 10:25). But we answer, "I just don't *feel* like going to church." We then stay home. Which voice speaks the louder? Which is supreme, our feelings, or God?

The merry-go-round will carry us to spiritual oblivion. We shall never reach the highlands of Canaan by riding it. We may wish to continue in circles. We may justify and rationalize our actions. We may fondle memories of God's blessings of the past and be content. We can only make progress when we stop the merry-go-round.

Not only does God command that we stop going in circles but He gives us a positive directive as to what we should do. To Israel, and to us, He says, "Turn ye northward." They had been circling Mount Seir but now the time for that had ended. Due north of them was Canaan wherein lay the great inheritance that had been promised to them. By going in a straight line they could reach it in a short while. His exhortation was that they visualize that goal and head directly toward it.

Beyond us lie vistas of beauty and experiences of depth. What we now possess is but a meager portion to what God would have us to inherit. He holds out his best to us and suggests drastic action to start us on the road toward it.

Stop the merry-go-round!

2

A Second Funeral for Lazarus

John 11:1-46

For the second time a funeral procession made its way to the cave on the outskirts of Bethany. A long time had elapsed since the first sad journey, but the body on the bier was the same one. Most of the sorrowing relatives had also made the first trip. The same professional mourners headed this procession and made the air resound with their shrieks and lamentations. Again they laid the bound and annointed body on the prepared niche in the cave and rolled a stone in front of the door. The body of Lazarus was laid to rest.

Lazarus was one of the few men who died twice. There is no record in the Scriptures of his second funeral, but there must have been one. The first time he died, his body stayed in the grave only four days. His Friend, Jesus, performed a great miracle and raised him from the dead. Lazarus had testified to what happened, and others also had faithfully attested to the miracle. They had extolled the power of Jesus Christ to raise even a body that was in a state of putrefaction. Now the testimony of Lazarus was silenced, for again death had overtaken him.

As his friends and loved ones slowly walked away from the grave, perplexing questions must have raced through their minds. How baffling were the doubts and misgivings that pried into their thinking. Puzzled minds must have entertained these and a host of other questions:

"What will the critics say now?"

"Will this discount the whole testimony of Lazarus?"

"Will he be raised again from the dead?"

"Why would God allow such a thing to happen?"

"Had Lazarus failed God?"

"Had God failed Lazarus?"

"Is the power of God limited because Jesus is bodily absent?"

"Why would a person sicken again after being healed?"

"Why would a person die again after being miraculously raised?"

The questions plaguing the bereft ones at the funeral of Lazarus have haunted people of all generations. The author of all doubts and the instigator of all unbelief would have us think God's power has failed because Lazarus died. He would have us despair because God does not always work in identical ways or manifest the supernatural at the very time we snap our finger. Such questions are like doubts intended to inflate faith and reduce our God to an impotent figurehead. Satan would have us believe such questions are insurmountable. At the time of apparent defeat he would make us believe that the cause is lost because Lazarus died the second time.

But to know God's Word is to know His ways. To know His ways is to resign to His infinite plan our limited understanding and to realize that "He doeth all things well." If we know and understand four basic rules of God's workings, we can dispel the haunting questions that come in our time of testing.

1. *God is not obligated to work in identical ways.*

As sovereign, God determines whether there will be a supernatural deliverance, when it will come, and how. We cannot draw boundaries for His power even by tracing the history of past events. He often deals with different individuals in different ways. He may deal with the same person in various manners at different times. There was supernatural deliverance for Paul at Philippi, accompanied by the rumble of an earthquake. Later, at Rome, he was not delivered but instead was given dying grace to go to the chopping block without flinching. Peter had a glorious deliverance from prison but later God let him die a martyr's death. Stephen had no unusual deliverance at all, but does that say he was loved less by our Lord? The disciples escaped from many plots against their lives, and yet eventually all but one of them suffered as martyrs. If God had done for all men what He did for Daniel and the three Hebrew worthies, there would never have been a martyr in the history of the church.

Neither God nor Lazarus failed when death struck the second time. It was for God's glory that Lazarus was raised the initial time but not any less so that he was buried the second time.

2. *Everything that is done for the body is temporal.*

At the very best, the human body is a brief abode for man. We are prone to exaggerate the value of the flesh and pamper it as though it were eternal. Because the ills or ecstasies of the body so vitally effect our spirits, we overrate its importance. The average man evaluates the body well above its counterpart, the soul, and even some Christians have a tendency to do the same.

Nothing we do for this body will endure beyond the disintegration that is inevitable. In that sense every physical healing is only temporal. It somewhat shocks us to realize that every person Jesus ever healed eventually died. There is no such thing as a permanent healing because healing has to do with that which is basically temporal. With that thought in mind, the burial of Lazarus is less of a calamity and does no discredit whatsoever to the power of God.

3. *The motivating purpose is more important than the miracle.*

Miracles have always played an important part in the plan

of God. We see them today as have the believers of all
generations. They are the hallmark of God's power in our
midst.

When viewed with the right perspective, the miracle takes
second place to the purpose that lies behind it. Christ miraculously fed the thousands but rebuked those who followed
Him for bread only. It is commendable to feed men, but He
had a higher aim than that — to give them the bread of
life. The loaves were but a means to a nobler end. Jesus
did not heal just to remove the aches and pains of men. To
do so is a splendid work, but His healing powers were
intended to open the door to the eternal soul. If we see only
His miracles, we lose sight of the more important motive
for them. If the aim could be accomplished by a miracle,
then a miracle was bestowed. If the purpose could be brought
about without it, then the miracle was superfluous.

Christ plainly declared that the sickness and death of
Lazarus was for the glory of God. If it was for God's glory
that he remained dead four days, could it not be conceivable
that he remain dead longer the second time? Whether or
not there was a miracle mattered little, as long as God was
glorified.

4. *Apparent defeat is often but delayed victory.*

Death takes every appearance of defeat. It seemed doubly
so at the second funeral for Lazarus. This could be the
crushing blow to the faith of so many. The body that had
been raised by the Lord was again in the grave. In human
reasoning, the hopes of many could be buried with Lazarus
in that grave. This looked like utter defeat.

Oh, that the ears of the bereaved could hear again the
words that previously echoed against that hillside. "I am the
resurrection, and the life: he that believeth in me, though
he were dead, yet shall he live." Jesus is gone, but the words
are still true. Lazarus is dead, but the promise is sure: "Yet
shall he live." Circumstances indicate defeat, but faith remains strong. Lazarus will yet rise from the dead. It might
not be within four days, as men would wish it; but rise he

will, because the Lord has spoken it.

In His first miracle, Jesus turned water to wine. He it was who devised a process by which a vine obtains moisture from the soil and makes it into grape juice. In the miracle He did not defy natural laws but rather just speeded up the process. When Jesus raised Lazarus, He did what He will eventually do for all believers. He did it a bit earlier for Lazarus, to demonstrate what all of us can expect. In spite of his dying again, he will be raised to die no more. What difference does it make to our Lord whether it be four days or two thousand years? The emphasis is not on the intervening time, but upon the fact of the resurrection.

The bereaved at the second funeral for Lazarus had the same hope as all who have lost loved ones in Christ. Satan may raise questions and inject doubts, but we stand upon the promise of our Lord: "Yet shall he live."

3

The Life of One Dimension

"And all the days of Methuselah were nine hundred sixty and nine years: and he died." — Genesis 5:27

As a lad, I puzzled long over a simple statement spoken in my hearing. Someone said, "The oldest man that ever lived, died before his father did." How could such a thing be true? If he died before his father, then the father would have the record for longevity. Delving into my Bible I found out that Methuselah lived longer than any other person on record and that his father was Enoch. Of course, Enoch did not die because he was translated. Thus a statement that appears to be untrue is really factual.

If Methuselah did not hold the age record his name would be little known to Bible students. It would have been buried with hundreds of other strange names in the musty genealogies and seldom called to mind. As it is, he holds one distinction only — that he lived 969 years. Some came near to that mark but never was it equalled or surpassed and it is unlikely it ever will be.

Methuselah came very near to the thousand year mark. Had he but lived thirty one more years (a mere trifle as compared to his life) his age would have run into four figures.

I wonder if he ever set his goal to live to be a thousand years old? Sometimes men set such goals. We strive to live as long as our parents, to the Biblical three score and ten, longer than anyone in our family or to just a ripe age picked at random. The late Bud Robinson used to say, with a twinkle in his eye, "Bless God, I'm going to live to be a hundred years old — or die in the attempt!" I wonder if Methuselah ever set or sought such a goal?

Whether or not he had such a goal Methuselah fell short of it. He came so near to living a millennium and yet he missed it. He lived a full life and was so close to a natural goal. Then he died. What eventually caused his death? He weathered the childhood diseases of measles, chicken pox and whooping cough. The afflictions that cut down others in their prime did not faze him. He was not in jeopardy as the pedestrians and travelers of our day. Did a stout heart finally give out or did the general weaknesses of old age overtake him?

There is a specific answer as to what caused the death of Methuselah. The average person does not know the answer, primarily because he never thought to look for it. An interesting experiment is to turn a group of Bible scholars loose in the book of Genesis searching for the answer. Some will find it readily and others will avow that it is not there.

You will know *how* Methusaleh died if you determine *when* he died. He came to his end by drowning. It all happened in the flood when his grandson, Noah, was spared. Just a little figuring will bring you to that conclusion. We are told that Methuselah was 187 years old when his son Lamach was born (Genesis 5:25). Lamach was 182 years old when his son Noah was born (Genesis 5:28). Then we know that Noah was 600 years old when the flood came (Genesis 7:6). Adding those three sets of figures brings a total of 969 — the span of years from the birth of Methuselah until the coming of the flood. From the birth of Methuselah until his death was also 969 years. Because of that, the majority of the Bible scholars and reference books are of the opinion that he died in the flood. Of course, there is room for a

difference of opinion. I will grant that he could have died
of a heart attack just an hour before the rain began to fall.
However, the most logical assumption is that, inasmuch as
he died at the time of the flood, he died in the flood.

When this knowledge first comes to a person he generally
reacts by saying, "Well, then Methuselah must not have been
a righteous man." There is not the slightest hint anywhere
in the Scriptures that he was righteous but all of us want
to believe so. Those who contend that he died just before
the flood do so primarily because they want to claim a righteousness for him of which there is no record. The most plaus-
able assumption is that Methuselah was a sinner and died
with the rest of the sinful world in the catastrophe of the
flood.

The life of Methuselah had basically but one dimension.
He lived a long time — even to setting a record for longevity —
but that is the best that could be said for him. The divine
record expresses it briefly, "Nine hundred sixty and nine
years: and he died."

Even with the limited knowledge at our disposal about the
man Methuselah there are some specific lessons for us to learn
from his failures. May his life speak to ours and cause us
to think deeply about factors that contributed to his downfall.

1. *There is more to life than just length of days.*

It is not enough merely to live a long time. In real living
there is breadth, depth and height. It is not only how long
you live but how well.

All of us know individuals who have lived over the century mark. They have been feted and honored for that one
accomplishment. In some instances that is the only reason
they are remembered in the community. No other accomplishment can be chalked up to them, just that they lived
a long life.

David Brainard, missionary to the American Indians is an
illustration of the reverse. He died at the age of twenty-nine
after having given his all to bring the gospel to others. His

few years were spent where the efforts counted for time and eternity. He lived a short time, but well.

A pastor called on a parishoner who had been an invalid for over thirty years. His sympathy got away with him as he said, "My, your world is small. For so many years it has been only this room." To which the beaming invalid replied, "Pastor, you are measuring only the length and width of the room. You forget the height. This room reaches to heaven."

There are hidden dimensions in life, too. He who sees only length is missing much in life. Even if he lives as long as Methuselah and overlooks the other dimensions he is a failure.

2. *Saving faith is not transmitted from father to son.*

Children inherit many things from their parents but faith is not one of them. They may receive training that will channel them into the paths of righteousness but personal faith is a different matter. Many hope against hope that a parent's faith will save them but it never has happened and never will.

If any son could ride into heaven on the coat tails of a godly parent, Methuselah would qualify. His father Enoch, walked with God so closely that he was just caught up to heaven without tasting death. He was a man of God if ever there was one. If anyone could get into heaven on the strength of having praying and devout forebears, then Methuselah could. In spite of that he drowned with the rest of the sinners.

You cannot inherit your father's education or degrees. Learning is a personal matter. You cannot insert your name in the citations of his military bravery. In spite of his heroism you can remain a coward. Your godly parent may want you to be saved but at his best he can only pray that you will make the personal decision of faith in Christ that will assure your joining him in the eternal city of God.

3. *The truth of God does not come by seniority.*

Noah, the grandson of Methuselah, heard the voice of the Lord, built an ark, and exhorted his contemporaries to seek safety from the impending flood. For 120 years he carried on that work while he was ridiculed by the general populace. The town rowdies kept up a constant din of jeers as they belittled Noah and what he was doing.

Can you not visualize Methuselah as a part of that crowd, expressing his feelings too? "I don't know what's got into the head of that grandson of mine. He's got some very wild ideas. He says there is going to be a flood. Such a thing has never happened and it never will. I've lived a lot longer than he has and I know more than he does. He's just a young fellow (in spite of being almost 600 years old) and what does he know?"

Noah was right and the crowd was wrong. The flood did come and calamity befell the mockers — including Methuselah. It is true that he was older, had more gray hair, and more experience in life but still he was wrong.

Age has nothing to do with God's truth. Seniority, experience, reasoning, natural wisdom or education do not have the pat answer about the workings of God. Noah had inclined his ear and heard God's voice and then acted in faith.

Men still laugh at the suggestion of impending judgment coming upon this world. They ridicule those who point to a way of deliverance. Human reasoning says such an event shall never transpire and men join the merrymakers and the scoffers. He who will incline his ear to the voice of God will faithfully declare God's truth and be vindicated. "As it was in the days of Noah, so shall it be also in the days of the Son of man" (Luke 17:26).

The life of Methuselah was not only of limited dimensions but one that was cut off by catastrophe. What he did not have we can yet attain through Christ, life more abundant and life everlasting.

4

What Did the Sheep Say?

I Samuel 15:1-3, 9, 13-15, 19-22

Is it possible for a sheep to speak to a human being? If so, what type of message would such an animal convey? Out of the ancient past comes an interesting incident that provides an answer to both these questions.

In any court trial each witness testifies under oath as to what he knows about the matter at hand. Often there is a parade of such witnesses — and many give contradictory testimonies. It is the responsibility of the judge or jury, to ferret out that which is the truth.

Recorded in the fifteenth chapter of I Samuel is an incident in which there are contradicting testimonies of what was, or should have been, done. Four voices were heard in the matter: God, King Saul, Samuel and — of all things — some sheep. Let us examine the testimony of each.

WHAT DID GOD SAY?

His instructions to Saul, the warrior king, were very clear. "Now go and smite Amalek, and utterly destroy all that they have, and spare them not; but slay both man and woman, infant and suckling, ox and sheep, camel and ass" (v. 3). This harsh action was ordered because of what Amalek did to Israel in the past and to forestall similar trouble in the future.

WHAT DID KING SAUL SAY?

Saul heard God's command and started to obey it. When he next saw the prophet Samuel he exuded all sweetness and piety in declaring, "Blessed be thou of the Lord: I have performed the commandment of the Lord" (v. 13).

WHAT DID SAMUEL SAY?

He did not condemn nor criticize but merely asked a simple question. "What meaneth then this bleating of sheep in mine ears, and the lowing of cattle which I hear?" (v. 14).

WHAT DID THE SHEEP SAY?

The sheep said, "Baa!" What would you expect the sheep to say? What else *could* they say? Strange as it may seem, that unusual and simple testimony clinched the conviction of Saul, who denied his guilt in pious tones.

In no way am I being facetious or flippant when I lay this emphasis upon what the sheep said. There is a full, well-rounded message in the "baa." Allow me to translate it into English so that you may get the message. I do not claim to be an expert interpreter of the language of animals but I am confident of the meaning in this case.

There are four major truths that the sheep declared publicly by their repeated bleating:

1. Baa! *"God's will has not been done."*

Contrary to what Saul had said, the command of God had not been carried out. The sheep that should have been dead were still very much alive. The apparently inarticulate utterance said more than Saul's pious words.

2. Baa! *"Saul's consecration is defective."*

He purposed to do God's will and claimed to have done so. An ulterior motive and selfishness sidetracked him. While failing God he attempted to cover up his glaring inconsistencies by honeyed words and vain excuses.

3. Baa! *"Saul's actions are different from his words."*

Basically he was a hypocrite, and the sheep brought about an exposé of what he really was. His boastfulness was but a facade and camouflage for his failures.

4. Baa! *"Saul is lying to the prophet of God."*

The very beasts he spared were the ones who convicted him of his disobedience. Then, to cover up, he lied and veritably took the name of God in his prevarication. The bleating of the sheep brought all of that to light.

In our generation, as in all others, we hear the bleating of sheep which expresses more than words or pious public actions. Perhaps ministers have their ears attuned to such sounds more than others. When the pastor enters, the conversation in the living room becomes spiritual while secrets are guarded from him in the back room. One such spiritual leader tells of being in a home where there was every outward indication of spirituality. While conversing in the living room, a son came in the back door with groceries and called out, "Dad, do you want the beer put in the refrigerator?" Baa!

Saul was trying to hide things from the man of God. Samuel was not looking for sheep. When he had no reason to doubt Saul, he heard the sheep bleat forth. A preacher is not a detective nor a snooper. Neither is any other really spiritual person. They do, however, have good ears to detect the bleating of sheep and the lowing of oxen. Unslain sheep and cattle just will not keep quiet!

What do the unslain sheep of our lives say to those round about us? Do they convict us of being hypocritical as they did Saul? Do they remind us of lies in our consecration vows, in our praying, singing or testifying? Do they openly contradict the words that we speak for the Lord?

Too often our outward show of spirituality is contradicted by the bleating of worldliness. Our claims to the virtue of humility are annulled by the lowing cattle of pride that has never been crucified — even to being proud of our humility. Theoretically, we have crowned Christ as Lord of our lives only to have the telltale sounds of selfishness say that all the animals have not been slain. We exhibit apparent interest in God's work but the bleating of indifference and unconcern mocks our sincerity. We own Christ as Master of our lives, only to have evidences of carnal habits sound forth at the most unexpected and embarrassing moments. All these things speak of defective consecration. Who can contradict the message of the bleating sheep and lowing cattle?

Knowing these things, what shall we do? Can we really fool God, or even those around us, by our continued self-justification? Sweet talk does not cover brazen disobedience. Saul was immature enough to try to lay the blame on others. It did not help him and it will not work for us either.

The best course of action is to put the bleating sheep upon the altar. God says, "Utterly destroy . . . and spare them not. . . ." Anything pertaining to the Amalekites has caused you trouble in the past and will do so again in the future. Having such an enemy calls for drastic action. Slay utterly. We must get the bleating stopped before we can get the blessing down.

Dead sheep do not bleat!

5

Message from a Moslem Mosque

With a sense of awe and respect we visited the historic Ommiad Mosque in the ancient city of Damascus. Our shoes were left at the door and we stood on the colorful Persian rugs while the guide explained the beauties of the mosque and the intricacies of the Moslem religion.

The prayer demands on the people are most stringent and exacting. Five times a day a call goes forth from the many minarets in the city. The first one is at four o'clock in the morning and others follow at noon, at three, five and seven in the afternoon. When the chant summons the people to prayer they stop all activity, wash their hands — if no water is available they go through the form with sand — and prostrate themselves facing the Saudi Arabian city of Mecca, birthplace of their prophet Mohammed.

Our Arab guide greatly impressed his Christian hearers with the Moslem responsibilities of prayer. We who were pastors inwardly wondered whether our people could or would follow such a schedule of devotion. Then abruptly he ended his presentation with a sentence that changed the whole matter. He said, *"But all the people do not pray."*

That casually spoken sentence has burned in my heart since that day. It weakened the whole picture of Moslem prayer

life, but the most realistic utterance that fell from the
lips of the guide.

In the intervening time I have mentally tried to change
places with that Arab guide. If a group of Moslem tourists
came to the church where I serve as pastor and wanted a
guided tour, what would I have to present to them? There
would not be the expensive building, the exquisite rugs, the
mosaics or minarets. I could tell them about our beliefs, our
services and practices. If they asked about prayer I could
tell them about its wonders and could back my statements
with many portions of Scripture.

1. *The Christian is commanded to pray.*

The Lord we love said, "If ye love me, keep my commandments." Then He and others, who wrote the Scriptures, commanded us to pray.

"And he spake . . . unto them . . . that men aught always
to pray."

"Watch ye therefore, and pray always."

"Praying always with all prayer and supplication."

"Continue in prayer, and watch in the same with thanks-
giving."

"Ask, and it shall be given unto you; seek, and ye shall
find; knock, and it shall be opened unto you."

"Let us therefore come boldly unto the throne of grace."

The commands to pray are many *but all the people do not
pray.*

2. *There are limitless possibilities in prayer.*

Only a brief meditation upon many references will open
the eyes of anyone to the potential in prayer.

"The effectual fervent prayer of a righteous man availeth
much."

"And all things, whatsoever ye shall ask in prayer, believing,
ye shall receive."

"If ye abide in me, and my words abide in you, ye shall
ask what ye will, and it shall be done unto you."

"And whatsoever ye shall ask in my name, that will I do, that the Father may be glorified in the Son."

"And whatsoever we ask, we receive of him, because we keep his commandments, and do those things which are pleasing in his sight."

Who can grasp the vast possibilities in prayer? *But all the people do not pray.*

3. *There are great privileges in prayer.*

The most humble person can communicate privately with the God of the universe. Who can imagine such a wonder? It is man who determines when such a time of communion both starts and stops. He initiates the action.

"Draw nigh to God, and he will draw nigh to you."

"The Lord is nigh unto all them that call upon him."

The privileges of prayer are beyond human comprehension. *But all the people do not pray.*

4. *God promises to hear our prayer.*

The exercise of prayer is not merely speaking into thin air. It is a matter of speaking to One who always has an open ear.

"The eyes of the Lord are upon the righteous, and his ears are open unto their cry."

"And it shall come to pass, that before they call, I will answer; and while they are yet speaking, I will hear."

"Then shall ye call upon me, and ye shall go and pray unto me, and I will hearken unto you."

We know that God hears our petition, *but all the people do not pray.*

5. *God promises to answer prayers.*

Prayer is not merely "getting something off your chest." It is more than a psychological release which makes us feel better. If the Bible is true (and it is) then we have the assurance that our prayers are answered.

"Then shalt thou call, and the Lord shall answer.

We have the promises that God takes action at our request;

we are encouraged to pray in every circumstance. *But all the people do not pray.*

None of us would deny these basic truths about prayer.

All of us believe in prayer.

All of us know we should pray.

All of us know the value of prayer.

All of us know how to pray.

All of us render lip service to prayer.

But all of us do not pray.

I wish I could tell my Moslem friends that we Christians are different in that respect. I would like to tell them truthfully that all our people pray — but I cannot. I would like to tell them that all those of my denomination pray — but I cannot. I would like to tell them that all who are in my church pray — but I cannot. Human nature is the same everywhere. With my Arab guide I can talk about prayer but must join him in saying, *"But all the people do not pray."*

I would like to change the situation but am helpless to do so. You may feel the same way. The best thing we can do is to make sure that we as individuals live up to every privilege and practice of prayer.

All the people may not pray — but I can. And so can you.

The disciples once said to Jesus, "Lord, teach us to pray." They were not merely asking *how* to pray, but *to* pray. We who are His disciples in this modern day can make the same request.

Lord, teach us to pray!

6

Remove the Blindfold!

II Kings 6:13-17

Why do men react differently in times of danger or difficulty? Some go all to pieces, get panicky, lose their heads and act most erractic. Others keep calm, cool, collected and unperturbed while under fire. Why the big difference? What do some men have that others lack?

An enlightening example of such a contrast is found in the Prophet Elisha and his servant. They lived together and shared much in common. Early one morning the servant arose to find, to his horror, that the city was completely encircled by the hordes of Syria. The sight of so formidable an enemy, posing a current danger, frightened him. He became excited, fearful and perplexed. Panic-stricken, he rushed to his master asking frantically what they should do. The bad news had a different reaction on Elisha. He remained calm and even admonished his servant to have no fear.

How could Elisha act like that in the face of such danger? Didn't he realize the seriousness of the situation? It isn't even natural for one to be so calm in the face of such danger.

What was the difference between the two men? Elisha's servant saw nothing but the invading army. His vision was limited. He saw circumstances only, and forgot about God. He saw the foe but not the guardian host which was also surrounding them. He saw the danger but not the protectors. Elisha saw the guardian angels and knew nothing could thwart the plan of God. He rested confidently on that assurance and said, "Fear not: for they that be with us are more than they that be with them." Elisha saw more than his servant could see.

The prayer of the prophet was practical and meaningful. He did not panic and call on God for immediate reinforcements. The heavenly troops were there and he knew it! Instead, he asked that the eyes of his servant be opened. "And Elisha prayed, and said, Lord, I pray thee, open his eyes, that he may see." He asked that the blindfold be removed so that the young man might be aware of the Lord's army standing on alert. The miracle of the occasion was not that God's hosts were surrounding them, but that the eyes of the servant were opened to see them. "And the Lord opened the eyes of the young man; and he saw: and behold, the mountain was full of horses and chariots of fire round about Elisha."

God's invisible hosts still surround His people. We have a spiritual escort to convoy us through the dangerous passageways. The role of God's angels is described in various parts of the Word of God. "Are they [angels] not all ministering spirits, sent forth to minister for them who shall be heirs of salvation?" (Hebrews 1:14). "The angel of the Lord encampeth round about them that fear him, and delivereth them" (Psalm 34:7). "As the mountains are round about Jerusalem, so the Lord is round about his people from henceforth even forever (Psalm 125:2). With such promises as these we need not call for help — we have it standing by. We have only to ask God to open our eyes to what He has already provided.

Elisha's servant does not stand alone in the Bible as one who had his eyes opened to behold the protective forces of the Lord. God opened the eyes of Hagar to see the very thing she needed most — water in the desert (Genesis 21:19). Balaam had a similar experience to recognize an angel who was keeping him from straying out of God's will (Numbers 22:31). Cleopas had his eyes opened to recognize that his companion was the Christ Himself (Luke 24:31). Many others have had parallel experiences.

The contrast between the actions of Elisha and his servant bring three pointed truths to us. In our times of crisis and danger we can bank heavily upon them.

1. *Faith opens our eyes.*

By faith we see the unseen, know the unknowable, and attain the impossible. Those who have no faith live in a very limited world. He whose knowledge comes only through his five senses is extremely restricted. Those senses which are supposed to be the means of our knowledge actually conceal more than they reveal. The person without faith is in a worse plight than he who is physically blind. Faith opens our eyes to see new vistas and understandings as it did for Elisha's servant.

2. *Faith keeps us calm in the crisis.*

Frenzy, anguish and outward distress are not evidences of a strong Christian faith. They are rather the marks of one who sees only circumstances and is overcome by them. He sees the enemy but not the Saviour. He supposes he must stand alone against the onslaught of the enemy. No wonder he gets frantic.

Faith holds us steady. He who has faith recognizes the presence of God and that He is sufficient for all things. He sees Him as overruling the most adverse conditions. He knows he has a God who is bigger than his enemy.

In the will of God, you need not fear when troubles come. See Him who is greater than circumstances and in that way remain calm. Even one person with God is a majority. Who can withstand such a partnership?

3. *Faith assures our safety.*

Both Elisha and his servant were safe from the enemy, because God's protective forces surrounded them. The difference was that one knew it and was calm while the other did not and was afraid. The sight of the angels and chariots of fire did not add to the servant's protection. He was as safe before his eyes were opened as afterwards.

The disciples thought they were in danger of sinking when in the storm on Galilee (Luke 8:23-25). When Jesus was awakened, they felt safer. What they did not realize was that they were safe whether He was awake or asleep. Such knowledge would certainly have added to their peace of mind.

When a host of enemies surround your camp, you can do one of two things. You can panic as did the servant or keep calm as did Elisha. Which you do will depend upon what you see. If you see only the problem, the difficulty or the obstacle, then you will be frightened and miserable. If you see the Lord and His surrounding angels, you will be a paragon of calmness and will be amazed at your own behavior.

Remember, you need not call for reinforcements in an emergency. Just ask God to remove the blindfold so you can see the ever-present help at hand. If doubts creep in, then say with the Psalmist, "Open thou mine eyes."

The Afterglow

"And it came to pass, when Moses came down from Mount
"Sinai with the two tables of testimony . . . that Moses wist
not that the skin of his face shone." — Exodus 34:29

You are sitting on a crag high in the Bernese Alps of
Switzerland. The sun has already dipped behind the western
peaks. Below stretches a vast panorama of beauty. You are
absorbed with the scenes and sounds of eventide — the rough
alpiner's shack, the tinkle of cowbells on the slope, and the
placid lake in the valley. It is a spectacle long to be remembered.

The sun has disappeared but light remains. The once-white
clouds blush from the parting kiss of the sun. The snowy
summits still reflect the sunset, and congregated hues of beauty
radiate from the crests and ravines. There is no visible source
of light, and yet a lingering phosphorescence covers the whole
majestic view. At such a time as this, the mighty Alps be-
latedly reflect the beauty of the sun and cling to it as if
reluctant to give up its effulgence. Men call it the afterglow.

Then your mind goes back to an ancient mountain scene
and another type of afterglow. You recall the rugged mount
called Sinai, between the two arms of the Red Sea. While

on its summit, Moses fasted forty days and experienced unin-
terrupted communion with God. Triumphantly he started
down the incline with the tables of the Ten Commandments.
In reporting this event the Scriptures say, "That Moses wist
not that the skin of his face shone." The literal meaning is
that his face "shot out rays" or was irradiated.

What made the mountain to glow even after losing contact
with the sun? What made the countenance of the prophet
to shine as he talked to his people? In both instances the
answer is the same. It was the afterglow. The snowy peaks
absorbed and reflected the rays of the sun; and Moses was
saturated with the white light of the holiness of God so that
it could not help but shine through his features. What a
glorious afterglow follows a tryst with God!

The radiant face of Moses was the hallmark of heaven. It
was the outgrowth of his communion with God and signified
that he was qualified to speak for God. To the Israelites it
gave a practical demonstration of the Glory of Jehovah. Our
reading of the account today brings to us certain aspects of
the holiness of God that cannot be overlooked.

Someone has said, "He who would know what glory is must
go where glory is obtained." God is the source of such a
radiance as Moses experienced. The shine of glory does not
come by merely withdrawing from the throng to an isolated
place. It is not the result of going through pious actions or
mouthing spiritual phrases. It does not come through buffing
or exterior application. Such holiness and radiance is a reflec-
tion of the brightness of God, and can only be gotten through
close and constant communion with Him.

The experience of Moses is a picture of all true spirituality,
in that he was unaware his face shone. The radiance was
seen and known by everyone but himself. He was so absorbed
in his contact with God and in bringing God's message to
the people that he was unconscious of the heavenly beauty
upon his countenance. It had never entered his mind that
his face would shine. He did not see the afterglow, because
he had seen the far greater glory of the Sun Himself. The

highest spirituality is that which is unconscious of itself. Beware of self-conscious spirituality!

There is a self-conscious humility that is merely a subtle species of pride, and there is a self-conscious spirituality that is only masqueraded carnality. When children begin to learn they are cute, they cease to be so. So it is with spirituality. When a man suspects he is spiritual, he begins to be carnal. The one who highly esteems his own spirituality is of low esteem in the eyes of discerning men and God.

Many of us are prone to check the pulse of our spirituality. We are tempted to look in a mirror to determine the degree of radiation from our countenances. Is it any wonder we see so little? Better far to be engrossed in God, and in our service to fellow men, and ignorant of any evidence of God's glory.

When the glory of God is manifest through an individual, the masses will not always be drawn to that person. Some people revel in any manifestation of God, but others seem to be repelled by it. Even of the people who knew God it is said, "And when Aaron and all the children of Israel saw Moses, behold the skin of his face shone; and they were afraid to come nigh him" (Exodus 34:30). The visible evidence of God's presence makes some people miserable. The holiness of God makes them acutely conscious of their sin. It could well be that Israel's recent idolatry haunted them when they saw the glory of God upon the face of Moses. That may have been the cause of their fear. It was only after Adam sinned that he was afraid and tried to hide from God. Some people will be drawn to a Moses with a radiant face, and others will flee from him.

The true child of God longs for a close communion with God. His motive is not to seek a shining countenance but to have fellowship with his Maker. The face that radiates is often a result of such a meeting with God. Oh, that we might have more shining faces — and less personal awareness of that shining!

8

Hallowed Desert Sands

"And he said . . . put off thy shoes from off they feet, for the place whereon thou standest is holy ground."
— Exodus 3:5

Delightful experiences with God often come at unexpected times and in strange places. The man of God, Moses, could readily attest to that fact. In a startling manner, God broke into the humdrum and monotonous life of a shepherd on the lonely Sinai peninsula. The methods He used were most unusual. First, there was the singular and inexplicable phenomenon of a bush that burst into flame and still was not destroyed. That mystery sparked the curiosity of Moses. It led him, through a chain of unprecedented events, into a hallowed sanctuary where God could commission him for his great task of the future.

God's call for reverence is most intriguing and fascinating. He demanded that Moses remove his sandals and tread unshod in the presence of Jehovah. The removal of the shoes was not uncommon. It was an ordinary practice of reverence in ancient times. The interesting facet of the whole episode is that natural sun-bleached sand suddenly became designated by God as holy ground. That which was very commonplace became hallowed in but a moment. Such transformation becomes worthy of our further thought and consideration.

What is holy ground? What locations upon the earth do men count as sacred? What pinprick upon the map has God designated as particularly hallowed? Are the evaluations of man and God the same? This experience of Moses, and other Scriptural incidents, should help us to answer these questions and to understand more fully the significance of sacred terrain.

From the beginning of time man has singled out certain places on earth as being hallowed for one reason or another. Every religion has its shrines and holy places. Christianity is no exception. The land where most Bible events transpired is commonly called The Holy Land. The Bible scholar who travels in the Middle East in the interests of the geography of the book is often nauseated when he comes to the famous landmarks. A shrine is built over the major ones, commercialism is rampant and even idolatry prevails. A gullible public stands awe-stricken at the supposed footprint of Jesus in concrete on the Mount of Olives. The tourist pays hard-earned money for water from the Jordan river, a little sack of dirt from Mount Zion or flowers from Bethlehem. A thriving business is carried on at the places which man has designated as sacrosanct. These locations have been presumed to have been holy because of events that transpired there centuries in the past. Does that really make them holy?

What type of terrain does God designate as being holy? On only two occasions does the Bible mention hallowed ground. In a third reference it is inferred. This experience of Moses at Mount Horeb is one. When the Lord confronted Joshua in the moonlight near Jericho he was told he was on holy ground and must remove his sandals (Joshua 5:15). When Jacob had his great experience with God at Bethel he exclaimed, "This is none other but the house of God, and this is the gate of heaven" (Genesis 28:17). Not any one of these spots had any scenic beauty, whatsoever. Nothing significant had happened there in the past (nor has anything since) which would set apart these desolate points as being particularly sacred. In each instance it was barren desert land which suddenly became holy in the eyes of God. It is significant that no shrine stands today at any of these places. Were we to know, and to stand upon, the exact spot where these patriarchs stood we would see or sense nothing unusual. The likelihood is that we would question whether such ground could ever be called holy. No claim is made that these spots are now sacred — but they were once.

How does a plot of ground become holy? Some would answer that it does so because God is there. That may sound plausible, except for the fact that God is everywhere. Is there any area of the globe where God is not near? Were God's presence the answer then no part of the earth would be more sanctified than another.

A study of the three Biblical times when God hallowed a given geographical spot points up three basic facts about holy ground. If we thoroughly understand them we can have experiences like these ancient men of God. We can also avoid the idolatry that parades as piety at the supposed shrines of Christianity.

1. *Holy ground is where God and man meet.*

The present tense of the verb is important. Our great mistake is to suppose that an area is hallowed because God and man met there in the past. Monuments, pillars and shrines mark the spot where something transpired in days gone by. Ground is actually holy only if something is taking place there *right now*. At the time God and man converse their meeting place is hallowed. It has not been before and does not necessarily remain so afterward. Man approaches such a meeting with reverence and with both an open ear and an open heart. God welcomes man's approach and uses such an opportunity to impart His guidance to him whom he loves . The creator and the creature are joined in a trysting place and even the parched desert sands benefit from that union. In such a meeting the man becomes closer identified with his great God. His heart is purified, his thoughts clarified, his being sanctified and he receives a commission for service. Reverence brings a new solemnity and counteracts carelessness, listlessness and levity. He leaves that spot a changed man, even as the elements of the ground were changed during the time of meeting. Man's advantage over the ground is that he is able to retain a portion of the glory, which soon departs from the sand.

2. *Any spot on earth can become holy ground.*

Wilderness terrain can become a meeting place for God and man. A waste mountain can be transformed into the mount of God. A hard pillow in a rocky, forsaken area can become the very gate of heaven and the open door to divine blessing. Geographical factors, natural beauty and past events mean nothing. When meandering man hears the call of God and draws nigh to Him, something happens to sanctify the whole area.

Thirty years ago there was a rocky cave on a crag overlooking Burbank, California. Day after day I trudged up there, Bible in hand, to spend hours in communion with God — both to speak to Him and to hear from Him. To me that is a hallowed spot — but only in my memory. The intervening years have changed the whole area and probably an expensive home now perches on that high point. I am sure I could not even find the place. The residents on that promontory may have a view of the city below but I had an insight into what was above.

Because that cherished spot no longer exists does not restrict my communion with God. Whether in a cloistered sanctuary or a cluttered closet I can meet Him face to face. In intervening years I have been sequestered with Him on a lonely island in Alaska, high on a crag in the Cascade mountains, in a cave in Italy, on top of Mount Calvary, in the Garden of Gethsemene and in the heavily wooded area of Finland along the Russian border. No spot was more important or more holy than another. Each was sacred ground at a given time.

You, too, can stand on holy ground. It may be a pensioner's hovel, a hospital room, a bench in a city park, a rescue mission or a little back room in the factory during the noon hour.

If the sun-drenched desert sands could become holy ground then any place on earth can be as well.

3. *Any spot on earth can cease to be holy ground.*

This is a truth we are prone to forget. History verifies the fact that many a nation has once enjoyed God's blessing and then lost it. This is also the sad story of some individuals. The bleak area that was holy ground for Moses is no longer so. Even were there a monument at that spot it would not make it hallowed. Erecting shrines does not make permanent the blessing of God at that spot. Only the continually meeting with Him there will perpetuate His glory and power in that area. A dead religion can do no more than memorialize the events of the past. He who has a vital experience with God need not be at any given place to meet God. His sanctuary is portable in that it can be wherever he is.

The altar at which you were converted is sacred only as long as you continue to meet God there. The little white church of your youth is hallowed only as you and others regularly meet God there. To make a display piece of the sites of past blessing and have no current meeting place with God is folly indeed. Even if you stand at the same spot but do not draw near to God your ritual is empty and useless.

How inspiring it is to realize that any place can be holy ground. How sobering to know that it can also cease to be. Whichever it is depends upon us and our reaction to the call of God.

9

The Dejected Hero

I Kings 19:1-8

It is only a short distance from the pinnacle of success to the slough of despond. The high-pitched emotions of a mountaintop experience often give way rapidly to a dismal sense of failure. How quickly Elijah, the hero of Mount Carmel, became the coward of the desert. The fearless champion of righteousness, radiating a sense of glory and triumph, suddenly turned into a cringing, cowering pessimist praying to die. What a change in but a few hours!

Perhaps it was well that the Negeb desert was 100 miles from Mount Carmel. Those who had witnessed the dynamic leadership of the prophet and heard his vibrant prayers could hardly have reconciled them with his cowardly actions and whimpering petition under the little broom tree. Likewise many Christians would not recognize their hero of the Sunday morning pulpit were they to see him late Sunday evening, disheveled, dejected, discouraged and disconsolate. Like those of old, they would proclaim, "How are the mighty fallen!"

The Scriptures declare Elijah was a man of like passions to ours (James 5:17). We are more likely to believe the episode in the desert than the mountaintop success. Yet both can be, and have been, ours. If the juniper tree trials must come then we had best learn to cope with them, both in ourselves and in others.

When we plummet from the pinnacle of ecstacy to the depth of despair it would be well for us to read again the experience of Elijah and better understand this dejected hero of Carmel. Particularly can we find consolation in observing God's method of dealing with Elijah in that critical period when he prayed that he might die. In scrutinizing God's dealings with the prophet we receive new assurance of His help directed to us. In addition, we learn how to help our friends and fellow laborers better in their hour of discouragement or despondency.

There are six basic steps that God took to guide Elijah through his desert experience.

1. *God did not answer Elijah's prayer.*

It was fortunate for Elijah, and it is for us, that God does not answer all prayers. At times rash, feverish, and impulsive petitions pass our lips. In His mercy, God knows what is best and does not grant our every request. God did not take Elijah's life, but He did recognize his need and saw that he was not alone in his despairing state.

2. *God sent an angel to minister to Elijah.*

A beautiful picture unfolds when the Scriptures say, "Behold an angel touched him." The angel was a heavenly messenger representing God. His presence indicated that God was concerned for Elijah. He came to him and stayed with him at a time when he needed help most. The Scriptural record is replete with instances of angels appearing when people were in need. An angel even came to strengthen Jesus when He was in Gethsemane (Luke 22:43). It is said of angels, "Are they not all ministering spirits, sent forth to minister for them who shall be heirs of salvation?" (Hebrews 1:14).

In our times of despondency God's angel is by our side, whether we recognize him or not. He is with us as much in the desert experience as on the mountaintop.

3. *God saved Elijah from his moods.*

All of us experience varying moods but some are more accentuated than others. Elijah dissipated his energies through brooding over his failures. Eventually he gave way to unbelief and was swept into a sea of despondency. There he foundered, unable to help himself. What he thought to be the remedy was not God's plan. God knew the dominating force of his moods and saved him from them.

4. *God used tact in rebuking Elijah.*

A part of the despondency that gripped Elijah stemmed from the physical. He had run 17 miles to Jezreel ahead of the chariot of Ahab. The journey to Beersheba and into the desert was on foot. The blazing sun beat down mercilessly and he was physically tired. Very often discouragement comes when there is no other cause than physical weariness. In addition, he was nervously spent and exhausted. The angel let him sleep, awakened him for a good hot meal, and then let him sleep again. There is therapeutic value in food and sleep. It is better than medicine. Elijah had asked for the oblivion of death; instead God gave him the temporary oblivion of sleep.

God gave food and rest to his servant first, then instructed and rebuked him later. Eventually He asked, "What doest thou here, Elijah?" and later directed him into the place of His will. Elijah's hurried action and impetuous prayers had gotten him off the track. Now God used tact and wisdom in redirecting his life and ministry.

5. *God urged Elijah to tell of his grief.*

God knew all that had led up to this experience. In spite of that He asked Elijah for a recitation of the details. The feelings of his heart gushed forth like water from an artesian well (I Kings 19:10). He told of his zeal, his work, his concern for the cause of the Lord, and then ended up pitying himself because he had accomplished little and stood all alone. Merely his telling of his grievances opened a valve in his heart that relieved pressure and made it possible for him later to listen to God and do His will.

6. *He corrected his statistics.*

One reason Elijah became so discouraged was that he left the work of a prophet to become a bookkeeper. He was trying to figure out how many souls had been saved under his ministry and how much good he had done. If you want a good case of the "blues" try doing the same thing. Elijah spent much time, added all the figures, and came up with a total of one — he alone was serving God. The Lord veritably told him his addition was all wrong. He, Jehovah, had added the same column of figures and it came to a far larger total. He said there were 7,000 who had not bowed to Baal and were serving the Lord. The correct statistics themselves were enough to raise Elijah's spirits immeasurably.

A wiser preacher, he heeded his calling after that and left the keeping of the records to the Lord.

The brooding prophet had a grossly distorted view of the situation and the circumstances. In his deep despondency, he was not thinking properly. His enemies looked bigger to him than God. The results of his ministry looked insignificant and his efforts seemed futile. He was ready to give up in despair.

Elijah was a man subject to like passions as we are. When we find ourselves thinking as he did, the lessons he learned can serve us in a practical way. God had a great ministry for him beyond the time he thought he should die. In the Lord's plan he was *never* to die. God has things in your future, too, that will far surpass your expectations.

What if Ahab and Jezebel do rage? What if enemies bay at your heels like hounds? What if you are tired of the struggle, disillusioned in your ideals, and disappointed in your fellow human beings? What if the demon of discouragement has whipped you?

Elijah's God still lives! He is still on the throne! What he did for Elijah He will do for you!

10

The Commander-in-Chief

Joshua 5:13-15

What would you do if you were pastor of a church and a man walked into your study declaring he was the pastor? What would you say if a stranger sauntered into your classroom and claimed he was the teacher? How would you react if you were the general of an army and an unknown person said he was that general?

Such things don't happen? It *did* happen to Joshua, who was the military and spiritual leader of the Israelites. His experience could well be a lesson for us.

At eighty-four years of age Joshua assumed heavy responsibilities. He became the commander of the armed forces and the civilian leader of the Israelites. Before, he had given advice; now he must make the decisions. Some men can never adjust to such a change and very few do so at such an advanced age. The new role called for vision, initiative, and great courage. Joshua had no elder statesman, such as Moses, upon whom to lean. How keenly he must have felt the load that was on his shoulders.

The city of Jericho was the first formidable object in the path of the Israelites and it called for the initial conflict with an enemy. Plans must be made for that battle. We can visualize Joshua furtively approaching the walls of that city of palms and, in the glistening moonlight, surveying the fortress. He was privately reconnoitering, sketching his strategy and maneuvers. His mind was engrossed in the problems of the battle. He walked around the city, thinking his own thoughts, making his own plans, and wondering how best to capture it.

Suddenly Joshua realized that he was not alone. An armed figure was towering over him with a drawn sword. It was surprising to meet anyone in that lonely place, but much more so someone with a sword in hand. Soldier that he was, Joshua would not be intimidated. He challenged the stranger, "Are you friend or foe?" That was a natural question to be asked of an armed man in enemy country. It left no room for mere neutrality but called for a clear-cut declaration of allegiance.

The answer greatly surprised Joshua. The stranger declared He was Commander of the Lord's host. What did that mean? Which was the Lord's army? Certainly it was not that of the heathen enemy. It could only mean the Israelites — God's people. Further, He said He was *Commander* of that army. Was that not the very position Joshua, succeeding Moses, had recently assumed? Who was this that was laying claim to his own position?

This was no imposter, but the Lord Himself. Joshua was aware of a divine visitation. God appeared similarly to his forebears, Abraham and Jacob and also to Moses. This time there was no dream, vision, or burning bush, but the Lord came to a gallant warrior in the guise of a human fighting man with a drawn sword. Here, on the border of the Promised Land, the first Joshua met the second Joshua, our Saviour. He who was the type met the antitype and it all happened in God's plan.

The attitude of Joshua was noble and exemplary. He removed his shoes, which was the same token of respect that Moses gave at the burning bush. He bowed in worship and then waited for orders from the One who was his superior. By that act he acknowledged that he was but second in command. He had come face to face with the Commander-in-Chief of the Lord's army. While waiting in His presence Joshua received the full plan for the forthcoming conflict (Joshua 6:1-5). Then together they executed the strange strategy of the battle of Jericho and the result was a glorious victory.

Through that unique experience Joshua was both encouraged and instructed. What a boon to have a great leader to bear the heavy responsibilities! The weighty decisions were not his after all. He had One to whom he could bring the problems and from whom he could receive practical help. When Joshua was demoted from commander to lieutenant commander, it was a great day in his life. His strength reached its apex when he realized who was actually Commander-in-Chief.

Out of the unique experience of Joshua come many lessons for us all. We, too, face formidable enemies in our personal lives. Like Israel, we are confronted with obstacles that appear insurmountable. He who was Joshua's Commander-in-Chief is ours as well. If we would be victorious we must meet, recognize, and fall prostrate before Him. It is not a matter of planning the strategy but of waiting to get the battle plans from Him. Three main lessons from the experience of Joshua are those that we should learn well.

1. *Realize His presence.*

As you wrestle with problems and obstacles, pause long enough to be aware of the Lord's presence. He knows your weakness and the strength of the enemy. He is more concerned for your victory than you are yourself. He has a strategy for victory and has all power at His disposal. Do not go into the battle in your own strength but depend greatly upon Him.

> "Standing somewhere in the shadows you'll find Jesus,
> He's the one who always cares and understands;
> Standing somewhere in the shadows you will find Him,
> And you'll know Him by the nail prints in His hands."

2. *Recognize His authority.*

The Lord is not merely a helper — He is the Commander-in-Chief. He is not one to approach only when you cannot solve a problem, but the Leader from whom to receive orders. He must have the supreme place. Your duty is to give him respect and worship. The key to spiritual victory lies in demoting yourself to second in command and letting Him make the decisions.

3. *React to His commands.*

Both the battle plans and the power to carry them out come from the Lord. We must keep an open line to Him and move when and how He directs. We do not set the pace but keep in step with Him. If we recognize that the battle is His, then we shall fight it with His implements and in His way. Our part is to keep alert and await his orders.

For Joshua and the Israelites the victory at Jericho came dramatically and gloriously. Jesus, our Commander-in-Chief, plans just such a victory for us. It is up to us to fit into His strategy and share in that victory.

11

Deliberate Delay

"Now Jesus loved Martha, and her sister, and Lazarus. When he heard therefore that he was sick, he abode two days still in the same place where he was." — John 11:5-6

Delay is one of the severest tests to faith. As such it plays a great part in the plan of God. Contrary to general opinion, a deferred answer to prayer is a help to faith rather than a hindrance. It is the *trial* of faith that is precious (I Peter 1:7). Untried faith is weak faith. God exercises a discipline through divine delay which we must understand, submit to, and from which we will receive benefit.

A concrete example of Christ's strategy of delay is given in the above text. Jesus not only delayed in going to the bedside of his sick friend, Lazarus, but he was deliberate in that action. In His reasoning, the delay would work for more eventual good than even quick intervention.

Three basic facts are evident in the record of Lazarus' illness. First, friends of Jesus are not exempt from suffering. Secondly, friends of Jesus call upon Him when in need. And finally, friends of Jesus do not always get an immediate answer to their requests. It is that last truth with which we are now vitally interested.

The deferred answer to our prayers often puzzles us. If the Lord is going to answer at all why does He not do so immediately? Has God heard our prayer? Is He too busy to answer us now or is He limited in some way? If God be God, none of these doubts are justified or questions valid. Then just why does He deliberately delay as He did with Lazarus?

Let us peep in on the scene in Bethany in that day of long ago. Lazarus was criticaly ill and breathing very heavily. Martha and Mary tiptoed around the house and spoke in hushed tones. They had sent word to Jesus — if only He would come now, all would be well. Periodically they would go to the door in the hope He was coming up the path. They asked children to stand on the brow of the hill to report anyone coming along the valley road from Jerusalem. Hours passed, then days and night — and still no Jesus. Had the runner delivered the message? Did Jesus realize the seriousness of the situation? True, He had been across the Jordan and away north. Certainly by this time He could have traversed those sixty miles from Bethabara. Why, O why, doesn't He come? Then the blow struck! Death claimed Lazarus. Four days later — long after the funeral — Jesus arrived. What a pity He was so late! Martha couldn't hide her disappointment and said, "Lord, if thou hadst been here, my brother had not died."

What would Martha have thought if she had known that Jesus intentionally stayed two days longer in Bethabara after receiving the message? He didn't drop everything and run southward when the message came. He wasn't excited or perturbed about the matter. He didn't even send an advance runner to assure them He was coming. However, instead of indicating His lack of love for the good folks in Bethany, it more clearly demonstrated his love for them. They couldn't have understood it at that time but, in a backward look later, they would comprehend the full meaning.

Jesus loved them and *yet* He lingered. He had love for both the deceased and the bereaved and His delay was best for all of them. The apparent disinterest he showed did not diminish, nor detract from, the love He had for them. It was all a part of His plan.

Jesus loved them and *therefore* He lingered. The delay was the proving of His love. He purposed to do more for them than anything the wildest flight of imagination could conjur up. The height of what the sisters expected was that He would heal Lazarus before death came. Jesus demonstrated that He could do it afterward. His plan was to work a miracle in His own time, by His own methods and for His own glory. The deliberate delay was a part of that plan.

Why did our Lord prolong the sorrow of those whom He loved so dearly? Why does He allow any suffering to be extended? Sorrow is prolonged for the same reason it is allowed to strike initially. It is a backdrop for the great victory God designs to accomplish. Delay has its part in it all. The look of faith says, "This sickness is not unto death but for the glory of God."

Through this incident Martha and Mary learned a new truth about prayer. They were made to realize that delay is not denial. Instead it is the trial of faith and an integral part of God's program to strengthen and enlarge faith. "The trial of your faith . . . being much more precious than gold" (I Peter 1:7).

Perhaps, like these sisters of Bethany, you have asked your friend Jesus to come upon the scene. Because the answer has not been forthcoming immediately, all the gamut of questions, doubts and uncertainties have raced through your mind. You, too, have wondered why the delay. You may have even buried your hopes as they did when they buried their loved one in that cave on the hillside. The request has not gone unheeded. He is not unconcerned. Instead there has been a God-planned delay. Accept the discipline of that divine delay and be assured that the matter is in God's hands. He doeth all things well — and in His own time.

Jesus arrived in Bethany on time! Mary thought He was late. Martha thought He was *too* late. Instead He arrived at the split second when He was most needed. He never comes too soon or too late. Heaven's big clock sometimes differs from our little watches. If there is such a difference, it is my watch that is wrong. Trust Him to know, not only what to do in your case, but when to do it as well. He makes even the delays, which we assume are catastrophic, to redound to His praise and glory.

During a period of delay the prophet Habakkuk was waiting for an answer from God. The word that came to him at that time could readily apply to us now. "For the vision is yet for an appointed time. . . . though it tarry, wait for it, because it will surely come."

God delays work for His glory and our good. What more can one ask?

12

Restrained Righteousness

"And being let go, they went to their own company."
— Acts 4:23

The Japanese have a saying that a snake is orderly and straight as long as it is kept inside a bamboo stick. When released, it wiggles and acts snaky again.

Many persons are perfect examples of righteousness as long as restraint is exercised upon them. They are like barrel staves in that they are held upright by external hoops.

An experience of Peter and John is an example of that very principle, except that it is in reverse. The compelling force that took them from jail to church is illustrative of an inner drive that leads some astray when restraints are lifted.

Peter and John had a brief jail experience. They were used of God in healing a lame man and then preached a straight sermon to the onlookers. The reaction of the crowd caused them to be arrested. The next morning they were brought before the authorities and were grilled and cross-examined. Peter used the occasion to preach another red-hot sermon. After that they were threatened and commanded not to preach in the name of Jesus, and then released. Then follows the intriguing statement of the text, "And being let go, they went to their own company."

A test of what is in the heart comes when restraint is lifted. Chains and locked doors kept these men of God from being in a worship service with their brethren. When they were freed they instinctively gravitated to their own crowd. The dictates of their hearts had full sway and they could go where they wanted to be. Had they been drinking men they would have been drawn to the crowd that numbs its senses with alchohol. Had they been criminals they would have felt the tug to the dimly lit rooms where the language of crime is spoken and criminal acts are conceived. Because they longed for God they ended up among those with similar inclinations — in a fervent prayer meeting.

True character asserts itself in the absence of restraints. Often the removal of such restraint brings some startling surprises. When the exterior props to righteousness are taken away from the hypocrite he falls flat and his real character is revealed.

There are many common restraints that serve well in keeping people in the straight and narrow way of living. They serve a purpose, but only to a limited end, and then they fail.

1. *The restraint of physical force.*

Locked doors kept these two apostles from the place and people they loved. They were so encircled that they couldn't possibly get out. Many children and some adults are so buttressed by godly surroundings that there is nothing for them to do but go to church and put on a show of piety, whether they feel to do so or not. Circumstances are such that they are veritably forced to frequent God's house and associate with the people there. The apparent righteousness is dictated by circumstances rather than from the heart.

No one suspects a lack or questions the religious experience of such a person until the circumstances change. Then suddenly, restraint is lifted, and the individual heads toward his own crowd as a homing pigeon would.

2. *The restraint of home.*

No greater example can be given of a wholesome re-straining influence for righteousness than the godly home. A child grows and develops in a spiritual atmosphere and gives every indication of living on that level throughout life. Then he leaves home. If that home has been his only prop to righteousness then his life will be drastically different the moment he gets on his own. Without the restraint of the past he will go to his own company, as dictated by his heart. The result may be sudden and mystifying to those who have known him for so long. The fault is not that he failed to get training and atmosphere but that he got only them and not a heart experience of righteousness.

A short while ago a mother proudly let me read a letter from her son. He had just joined the Air Force and was taking his basic training. He wrote, "Mother, I'm having a new experience. For the first time, I am away from home. There are many temptations to wickedness and evil. There is no on to tell me I can't go certain places or do certain evil things. I am on my own, In spite of that I find no interest in those things. I would rather be in church and have found a very excellent one here where I can worship. Thank you, mother, for leading me into a heart-felt experience with the Lord that is just as real away from home as it is there."

That young man experienced more than the restraining influence of the home. In a far-away city his heart drew him to God's house. With the restraint lifted he found his own people — God's people.

3. *The restraint of associations.*

Good friends and loved ones are a wholesome influence and tend to prop us up in the things of righteousness. When we are hemmed in by a circle of such friends we can do hardly anything but stand. The big test comes when some of those loved ones and associates are no longer with us. Do we stand just as erect at such a time?

Two young girls never miss church and are always together. Then one goes away to college and the other never is seen in God's house. What happened? A young couple were very devout and spiritual. Then one day he was killed in an industrial accident. Now she runs with another crowd and forgets the things of God. What happened to her experience? Did she ever have one? The sudden, surprising changes in people ofttimes come when the restraining influence is lifted and the true dictates of the heart are in evidence.

4. *The restraint of tasks.*

All of us are conscious of the subtle dangers of idleness. The basic practice of many churches is to put all newcomers to work and use the energies of every person possible. The responsibilities of a job are the restraining force toward righteousness in certain types of individuals.

Then comes a test when a given work or position is taken away from that person. Often it is enough to tip the balance and that person becomes conspicuous by his absence from the house of the Lord. It is generally believed that we find out what is in a man when he is given a big job to do. Actually, the reverse is true. His true character is more apt to be seen when you take that job away from him.

At the very best, any exterior influence for righteousness is limited. The good powers of physical force, the home, associates and heavy responsibilities have their role, but also their limitations. They are but temporary holding actions intended to be steps toward the real source of righteousness — a changed heart. The righteousness that stems from them alone will eventually be shown up to be only veneer.

These truths point up the basic fact that only a changed heart can produce a truly changed life. The fountain of real righteousness flows out from within and not the reverse. We fail miserably if we only hold out to men the outward trappings of right living without presenting the need for, and possibility of, a complete inward transformation by the power of Christ.

Peter and John had just such a heart experience. They yearned for the atmosphere of prayer because the desire for prayer was deep within. Their crowd was the prayer meeting crowd. They were misfits in another atmosphere and only restraining force could keep them there. "And being let go, they went to their own company."

Which crowd is your crowd? Are you kept in the paths of righteousness merely by restraint or because your heart yearns for the fellowship with God and His people? Through Christ you can have a real change of heart that will make His people your people for both time and eternity.

13

The Underprivileged Failure

Matthew 25:14-30

A vast segment of humanity is classified as underprivileged. A person in that category does not start with the advantages enjoyed by his fellow human beings. He is often looked down upon and counted as being inferior. At times he is tempted to feel he didn't have a fair start in the race of life. Then self-pity takes over and plays havoc with both his present and his future.

Even worse, is the man who is dubbed as a failure. He is the person who aimed at success but fell far short of it. He may be ambitious, conscientious and a hard worker but still a failure. When the combination of these two is found in one life the results are even more devastating. To be both underprivileged and a failure is indeed humiliating and discouraging.

In one of His parables Jesus told of just such a person. He related the story of three men and how they handled money that was entrusted to them. Each man was given a different amount. One was given five talents, another two and the third but one. The talent was an ancient weight and unit of money which was of varying value. Through this parable the word has come into the English language and has come to mean natural endowments entrusted to us by God.

Our Lord's purpose in this parable is to illustrate the basic law of stewardship. Three cornerstone facts are that the talents belong to God, each man is given freedom in handling them, and each is responsible to report on his gains.

The five-talent man represents the person who has everything and is a success. The two-talent man is typical of the average man, with medium abilities, who is also to be commended for his accomplishments. It would be fascinating to delve into these success stories and find out their secrets. Instead, however, we shall examine their counterpart, the one-talent man. He was underprivileged in that he received a lesser gift and he was a failure according to the condemnation that came from the lips of Jesus. Perhaps his mistakes will point up more vividly the basis of stewardship than would the noble actions of the others.

The punishment of the one-talent man was severe indeed. He was rebuked publicly by the Lord and that must have been most humiliating. Eventually, the only talent he had was taken from him. Then he was cast into outer darkness. What an atrocious thing did he do to merit such judgment?

He did not do some things of which others were guilty in the parables of Jesus. His crime was not that of wasting the goods of the master as did the unjust steward (Luke 16:1). He did not live a riotous life as did the prodigal son (Luke 15:13). Neither did he go ten thousand talents into debt as did the unmerciful servant (Matthew 18:24).

His one offense was that he hid the talent. Because of a cautious spirit he did nothing at all and was condemned through that inaction. It was the failure to use his talent that made him a failure in every other way.

Although this man was both underprivileged and a failure, one had nothing to do with the other. Being underprivileged did not make him a failure. Being a failure did not result from his being given only one talent. Had he received five talents and done with them what he did with the one he would still have been condemned. With only the one talent he could still have been a success. *The number of talents initially entrusted to us has nothing whatsoever to do with our success or failure.* When we learn that secret we have a firm understanding of God's plan of stewardship. *It is what we do with the gifts of God that will make or break us.*

The basic aspects in the failure of this man are very evident. They stand out as a warning to every one who reads about him in the Scriptures.

1. *He had equal opportunities with the others.*

Although the endowments were unequal the possibilities were identical. Each man was obligated only for the amount entrusted to him. Enough time was alloted so that each one could double his investment. The final figures dealt not with the total but with the ratio to the initial gift. If the others doubled their amount he could have done the same. The two-talent man was not condemned because of not having ten talents but commended for having four. The one-talent man had just as much opportunity to hear similar words of praise from the Lord.

2. *He was possessed by a failure phobia.*

"I was afraid," he wailed, when reprimanded for his failure. The fear of failure was actually what made him one. The possibilities of failure loomed so large he had no opportunity to think of success. This debilitating complex haunted and veritably paralyzed him. As a result he did nothing.

If you do not venture for God for fear of making a mistake, you have already made a serious one. The supposed sensible caution that you exercise is motivated by a failure complex rather than by what you would prefer to call good judgment. In this instance what the man feared came upon him. He feared failure and thus became a failure. Burying the talent so that he would not lose it was the very cause of its being taken from him eventually.

3. *He was plagued with the blight of self-pity.*

There is no more subtle and yet destructive force than self-pity. It works on the human spirit as termites eat a wooden foundation. In the case of the one-talent man the stage was all set for self-pity to take over.

Others had received more talents than he. That means the master must have been partial and greatly disliked him. Then he would question the whole system of distribution. Giving more to one than another was completely unfair. In the next stage his thoughts would vent anger on those who received greater gifts. He envied them and wondered why they were better than he. The whole process left him thinking he had been mistreated, he didn't have a chance and he had better make sure he didn't lose the one talent.

One of the facts we must face is that in life we are given varying endowments. The mature Christian thanks God for his talent and uses it to the best advantage for God's glory. The person destined to be a failure whines and complains and justifies himself in doing nothing.

4. *He had a tight-fisted financial policy.*

The cautious soul that buries his money in a jar in the back yard will never become rich. Instead, he will become miserly and wizened in his attitudes and outlook on life. He runs no risks. Banks may fail. Some have lost their savings in an investment. Many hideous things can happen. He just plays it safe and hides his money.

The successful man in the business world makes money because he puts it to use and is willing to run risks. He that is used of God follows the same policy. Instead of a tight fist he has an open hand in both his investments and his giving.

5. *He made a long speech of justification.*

The one-talent man must have anticipated that he would be censured for his actions. He evidently had spent much time thinking what he would say for he had a pretty little speech on the tip of his tongue. He claimed to understand the master, what he wanted and then paid him a high compliment. He spent time thinking up excuses for his strange action rather than actually doing something. He falsely supposed that words are a substitute for deeds. The Lord turned his high sounding words right back at him and made them condemn rather than justify him.

The underlying truth of this parable and a basic principle of all life is summed up in three words — *use or lose*. If you strap your arm to your side and keep it inactive you will soon lose the use of it. That was true of the talents in this story Jesus told. It is true of the abilities and gifts God bestows upon us. The one requirement of a faithful steward is that he use all that God entrusts into his care.

> All that I have, all that I am,
> All I shall ever be;
> Cannot repay, the love-debt I owe,
> I surrender to thee.*

* Copyright V. B. Ellis, P.O. Box 788, Atlanta, Georgia

14

A Crusader, But . . .

"Thus Jehu destroyed Baal out of Israel." — II Kings 10:28

But Jehu took no heed to walk in the law of the Lord God of Israel." — II Kings 10:31

There is a strange inconsistency in the inspired record concerning King Jehu. These two statements, which are so near to each other in the Bible, appear to be contradictory.

Could both of these statements possibly refer to the same man? One verse commends Jehu for his righteous reforms, and the other points up his personal sinfulness. How could such traits be found in one individual? Is it possible to fight sin and still be a sinner? Can one successfully eradicate false religions and yet remain in a spiritual vacuum?

The experience of Jehu crystallizes certain facts and possibilities in that area.

A graphic weakness in human nature is depicted in these two cryptic statements from the Scriptures. The average person supposes that, when one is fighting evil, he is at the height of an effective work for God. We have been led to believe that breaking idols is serving the Lord. The experience of Jehu is a pointed reminder that merely blasting idolatry is a limited ministry with questionable results.

To the casual observer, Jehu was a great crusader for righteousness. He unsheathed his sword and slew all the household of Ahab because they had been idolaters. By the age-old trick of feigning to join the ranks of his enemies, he assembled all of the prophets of Baal to worship, and then he ordered every one of them slain. On one occasion he said, "Come with me and see my zeal for the Lord." The climax came when he was commended by God for what he had done (II Kings 10:30). He was imbued with a spirit to battle the things of Baal, and nothing could deter him in that campaign. Because of his efforts, the national worship of Baal in the northern kingdom was forever suppressed.

The pivotal word in these utterances is the little conjunction "but." It negates the first statement — or at least weakens it. The situation is comparable to that of Naaman of whom it is said, "Now Naaman . . . was a great man . . . *but* he was a leper." To read of the zeal of Jehu in combating idolatry is thrilling indeed. To view the success of his endeavor brings the greatest admiration for him. Then comes the word "but" and the whole complexion changes. He is still a battler against wrong, but his motive is open to suspicion when his indifference to the things of God comes to light.

Jehu was a crusader, *but*. He had a burning passion to destroy Baal and idolatry *but* he was unconcerned about the things of God. He could be commended for his campaign *but* he didn't go far enough. He implemented the negative aspect of a good cause *but* failed to emphasize the positive. He was a destroyer of Baal *but* not a servant of Jehovah. He was a zealot in tearing down superstitious beliefs *but* did nothing toward building faith in God. He reigned longer than any of his predecessors *but* his warfare against idolatry did little to arrest the downfall of the nation.

The crusade of Jehu had religious overtones but the foundation was definitely secular. There is every evidence that the motive was political rather than spiritual. He had energy and ambition, and channeled them against something evil instead of for something good. He merely fooled himself and a few people into thinking he was doing something for God, when in reality his heart was far from Him.

The tendencies of Jehu are so much like ours that his failures should be a pointed reminder to us. A person can fight the devil a long while without preaching Christ. *There is a temptation to join the wrecking crew rather than the builders, because it appears they are doing things faster.* It is easy to get fired up in a crusade against some evil practice and be so engrossed in it that constructive righteousness is forgotten.

There are innumerable evils in this world that should be eradicated. The liquor and narcotics traffic are blights upon our fair land. It arouses a man's fighting blood to see the havoc they play with our youth. Many a person has devoted every ounce of his energy to combating such vices. Surely God would delight to see all such things stamped out, as would all who view the problem objectively. We must be reminded, however, that merely fighting alcohol and dope has no constructive counterpart and is no substitute for personal righteousness. In this field many a crusader has falsely supposed that his tirades against the whiskey bottle have brought him the approbation of God.

Atheistic communism is the sworn enemy of God and righteousness. It has closed the doors to mission fields, boarded up churches, martyred the faithful, and substituted its propaganda for the truth of the gospel. So subtle are its tactics and so insidious its methods that Christians rise up with might and main to combat these hordes of hell. That, of itself, is good, but some have lost sight of the true objective. As in the case of Jehu, the crusade takes on political overtones and the cause of personal righteousness is forgotten. Just to combat communism is not enough. Not every fighter against communism is in the army of the Lord, nor does smashing something evil make the crusader a servant of God.

A person cannot become spiritual merely by abstaining from things sinful. Neither can there be a true spiritual crusade by only fighting that which is evil. The same principle holds for the individual or the world. It is good to put off the things of sin, but we must also put on the garments of righteousness. Fighting the devil is not enough; we must embrace Christ and present His glorious truths.

Sometimes we choose the easiest method that gives a semblance of accomplishment. *It is easier to fight than to build.* It is easier to use carnal weapons than constructive ideas. The first inclination is to pick up the hatchet, like Carrie Nation, and smash that which is offensive to us. Jehu shattered the idols that represented opposition to God but didn't make the positive moves that would make him acceptable to Jehovah.

The efforts of Jehu were largely wasted because they centered in the negative exclusively. He was a crusader, *but* he took no heed to walk in the law of the Lord.

The sound of the breaking of idols delights the ears of God, but the idol-breaker cannot enjoy His favor without personal obedience and holy living.

15

Subtle Slumber

"Watch ye therefore . . . lest coming suddenly he find you sleeping." — Mark 13:35, 36

The warnings of Jesus are often startling and surprising. He saw lurking dangers we would little suspect and pitfalls of which we are unaware. At times He was more concerned about thoughts than acts, motives than deeds and sleep rather than sin.

One such trenchant warning followed His Olivet discourse. He had told of the future destruction of Jerusalem and of His return to the earth again. Then he related the parable of the fig tree and sounded the need for watchfulness. Suddenly, He cautioned against a grave peril which would seem to us to be but a minor matter. To four of his most faithful disciples He sounded the warning of the above text.

There is a sinister peril of sleep that endangers even the most devout. Its approach is subtle, as that of a mountain lion, and its havoc as deadly. We count such slumbering as a natural tendency of mature years while He sees it as treacherous quicksand.

Our Lord did not count it necessary to alert His disciples against more evident evils. He said nothing about being found in acts of gross sin or frequenting hell-holes of iniquity. He evidently did not fear that they would be teaching error or rebelling against the truth. He didn't seem to be perturbed about the possibility of their consorting with evil companions or being completely backslidden. These are all recognized dangers. He was vitally concerned, however, lest they be found sleeping. He sensed a tendency toward drifting into a spiritually numbed condition and being found in that state at the time of His coming.

We would be naive to assume that such a warning to disciples in the first century does not pertain to us in this age. In times like these the dangers are even greater. The spirit of drowsiness encroaches upon us most subtly. Let us examine some of the avenues by which it comes.

SLUMBER BORN OF FAMILIARITY WITH THE TRUTH

It is possible to live with truth until it becomes commonplace. That which once challenged and alerted us now tends to have a soporific effect. We have become accustomed to the alarm until we are oblivious to its clanging. We have heard so much of the gospel until we have become satiated with it. We know the words by memory and can anticipate the thoughts and the admonitions. What can this younger generation of preachers tell us? We have heard the spiritual giants of the past and know all there is to know about the matter. The Biblical truths are no longer startling, spectacular or novel. The very truth that should awaken us lulls us to sleep. In this instance familiarity breeds slumber.

SLUMBER BORN OF A CLOSED MIND

A new convert searches eagerly for all truth, including doctrinal cornerstones upon which to build his faith. Too often he establishes his basic beliefs, puts them in permanent form, and files them away. From that time forth they are like the laws of the Medes and the Persians — unchangeable. He knows what he believes and will not discuss any other point of view.

Such a closed mind contributes to spiritual stupor. It receives no challenge and provides no mental exercises. A drowsy condition sets in, bringing beautiful dreams of being right while all others are wrong. A closed mind is a sluggish mind. It prompts one to say, "I have all the truth, please do not disturb me." As a lost person dying on the prairie in a blizzard, such an one sleeps to his doom amidst beautiful dreams.

SLUMBER BORN OF SUCCESS

It is said that Americans bow at the shrine of success. According to current thinking, anything that smacks of success must be right. Such a philosophy has even slipped into the church. The problem in such thinking is that there are varying standards of so-called success. What man calls success is not necessarily what God accepts as such.

We revel in statistics, balanced budgets, building programs and outward fanfares of progress. Even while taking bows for doing things for God we tend to become complacent and rest on past laurels. The dazzle of prosperity blinds us and we doze at a time when we should be awake. The more we receive the plaudits of men the greater the tendency to become oblivious to spiritual needs and thus become drowsy.

The Laodicean church saw itself far differently from God's evaluation. It said, "I am rich, and increased with goods, and have need of nothing." God said of that church, "Thou art wretched, and miserable, and poor, and blind and naked." The glare of apparent success subtly lulls us into deep sleep.

SLUMBER BORN OF UNCONCERN

There is no greater opiate to the church than unconcern. How easily we become wrapped in the cocoon of self-interest. In that drowsy state our senses become dulled, our reflexes sluggish and we drift into a spiritual stupor. We are saved and so is our immediate family. What else do we want? Our church building will accomodate our members and their families why should we enlarge it? We have a good class of people, why try to bring in some of the riff-raff in the immediate neighborhood?

Our eyes droop, our strength is wasted and our energies are useless because of unconcern.

SLUMBER BORN OF SHEER LAZINESS

The more one sleeps the more he feels he must sleep. Laziness spawns sleep and even the need for sleep. Eventually such a person has no ambition and no incentive but the height of his desire is to experience the nirvana of sleep.

That which brings physical sleepiness does the same in the spiritual realm. Sheer laziness causes many of us to slumber when we should be wakeful.

A classic story is told of a lazy hillbilly lounging in the shade in front of his mountain cabin. His wife called from the porch saying, "Pa, there's a funeral procession passing on the road." To which he replied, "I wish I were facing in that direction so that I could see it."

That story is a ridiculous picture of Christians whose water-thin excuses keep them from working for God. What a catastrophe to be found sleeping at His coming because of simple laziness.

Not only did Jesus warn against the danger of sleeping but gave an admonition to ward it off. He said, "Watch ye therefore." Watchfulness and prayer are repeatedly linked together in the Scriptures. One is an activity earthward and the other a petition heavenward. Being warned of a danger, excercising continual diligence, and remaining alert are steps toward skirting the pitfall of which Jesus spoke so emphatically.

The message of the Highway Department to the modern driver is God's message to us. The turnpike has leveled the hills and straightened the curves of this great land. Now the prime danger is that the driver doze at the wheel and destroy himself by going off the road. Removing other dangers has precipitated this one. For hours the driver has directed the car with hardly a turn of the wheel or changing speed. A robot could do that kind of driving. His eyes become heavy, his brain sluggish and he is near the danger point that has killed many a driver and his passengers. Suddenly he receives a message from the Highway Department. Gigantic yellow letters leap up at him from the concrete itself saying, "STAY ALERT." He perks up, opens a window, turns on the radio or starts singing. It could well be that his life has been spared.

Even more important than a mortal life is an eternal soul. JESUS IS COMING. STAY ALERT.

16

When the Twin Missed Church

"Thomas, one of the twelve, called Didymus, was not with them when Jesus came." — John 20:24

What happens when people miss church? What *makes* them miss church? The answers are found in the experience of the first man to absent himself from a gathering of Christian believers.

It was an Easter service; but even so, there was not perfect attendance. One church member found an occasion or excuse, to stay away. He had reason later to regret it very much.

It was a Sunday evening service, just hours after Jesus had risen from the dead. The meeting of the disciples was being held behind closed doors for fear of the Jews. Suddenly, Jesus appeared in their midst. He was making good the promise he had made when He said, "For where two or three are gathered together in my name there am I in the midst" (Matthew 18:20). He pronounced His benediction upon them, showed them His hands (which bore proofs of His resurrection), proclaimed a great message to them, renewed their commission, and bade them to receive the Holy Spirit (John 20:19-23). All of this caused the disciples to rejoice and be glad. It was a blessed meeting because the Lord was there.

But one of the eleven disciples did not share all those blessings. He was Thomas, who had every right to be there, but chose not to be. When we analyze the folly of his missing church we are reminded of our foolishness in doing the same thing.

Thomas is one of the most misunderstood men in the Bible. Extremists have dubbed him as either an unbeliever, because of his doubts, or a too-practical man because he was not inclined to be hoodwinked. Perhaps the truth lies between the two extremes. He had a sort of nickname that was often added when his name was mentioned. "Thomas . . . called Didymus." Didymus is a Hebrew word meaning *twin* and it is carried over without change into the Greek. It is generally believed that Thomas was a twin and this nickname was often used to set him apart from others with the same given name.

From certain experiences of Thomas we determine that he had traits which many of us have. He was easily despondent (John 11:46). He often saw the difficulties of a problem rather than the solution (John 14:5). He was opinionated and obstinate. He set his own opinion against what others had definitely seen. He said, "I will not believe, except. . . ." His self-reliance became conceit when he thought the touch of his ten fingers was more accurate than the word of his ten friends! He was a zealous, inquisitive, and somewhat incredulous man who found it hard to grasp the supernatural.

Whatever the good or bad traits of this twin, he made a serious mistake when he absented himself from church. He missed seeing Jesus and missed hearing the first message after His glorification (Luke 24:44-49). He missed the Lord's outbreathing upon the disciples; he missed the displaying of the evidence of the resurrection, and the salutation of peace that came to those who were present. Thomas needed all those blessings badly and he only did harm to himself by not assembling together with the others.

Why did Thomas miss church? Was it because he was afraid of the Jews? Had he been through so much that he was tired and needed rest? Was he discouraged? Was he disillusioned? Did he have so many things to do that he could not get there? Are such things as these — or inclement weather, a long distance to church, or unconcern — worth forfeiting what others may experience when they gather together? Are any of the excuses, hurriedly concocted to rationalize our absence from church, worth the spiritual losses that we thus incur?

It is no wonder that Thomas was plagued with doubts. His companions receive a glorious experience and all he got was a report of it — and he found that hard to believe. He was slow, suspicious, critical and skeptical. He even questioned the honesty of his friends. Instead of rejoicing with them he nursed questions and doubts, and those mental perplexities bring just the opposite of joy. Perhaps he wondered why he did not feel the joy that the other disciples seemed to feel. The difference was not inherent in the individuals; it lay in the fact that the other ten had been to church and he had not.

For an entire week the disciples were rejoicing while Thomas remained lonesome and cheerless in his melancholy musings. He was plagued by miserable doubts and his morbid meditations robbed him of a victory that could have been his. Missing church just made him critical all week. With such an attitude of heart Thomas could least afford to be alone. How unfortunate it is that those who can least afford it are the ones who most often miss the gathering of believers and suffer as a result.

The next Sunday Thomas was where he should be when the believers assembled together. Instead of staying away from church to brood over his troubles he came to have them dispelled. This time he saw the Lord! It was a transforming experience. He received the peace of the Saviour; he touched His wounds, and all his doubts were settled. He had a renewed conviction of the deity of Christ and shouted, "My Lord and my God."

Thomas believed one week later than did his fellow disciples. That intervening week was not one of joyful optimism but of morbid skepticism. Had he gone to church that first Easter it would have been different. Staying away from church did not solve his problems but rather added to them. The experience he received a week later could just as well have been his earlier if he had been with the others as they assembled together in the name of the Lord.

The experience of Thomas can well be a reminder to us. When a person is discouraged or tired is the very time to go to church rather than to stay away. The writer of the Book of Hebrews sensed this very truth when he wrote, "Not forsaking the assembling of ourselves together, as the manner of some is; but exhorting one another: and so much the more, as ye see the day approaching" (Hebrews 10:25). Instead of tapering off in church attendance as we grow older, or as pressing duties increase, we stand in need of attending church more often. As world conditions become more perilous, wickedness more prevalent, and the coming of the Lord approaches, we need to assemble in God's house more often than ever.

Thomas made a grave mistake when he missed church. We should profit by his experience.

17

The Blunted Thorn

"And lest I should be exalted above measure through the abundance of revelations, there was given to me a thorn in the flesh, the messenger of Satan to buffet me, lest I should be exalted above measure.

"For this thing I sought the Lord thrice, that it might depart from me.

"And he said unto me, My grace is sufficient for thee: for my strength is made perfect in weakness."
— II Corinthians 12:7-9

The barbed thorn that is now the bane of your life can become a source of true blessing.

That which you now count as "the messenger of Satan" can become an instrument for God's glory. Your mournful dirge can be changed to a paean of praise, and it will not take a miracle to bring it to pass. You have the power to fashion such a transformation. By one simple action you can dull the point of that which causes you pain.

Although this sounds like some occult philosophy of the current decade it actually stems from the Bible itself and is soundly orthodox. A magnificent example is found in the experience of Paul, the Apostle. Like you and me, Paul had a thorn in the flesh. See him with a painful, visible, humiliating, chronic affliction and then observe the transition that enables him to say, "I take pleasure in infirmities, in reproaches, in necessities, in persecutions, in distresses for Christ's sake" (II Corinthians 12:10). He found a way to blunt the thorn that had previously made him miserable. It changed from a curse to a blessing. The plan that worked for him can do as much for us.

What was the thorn that plagued the life of the illustrious Apostle? No one knows for certain. In Paul's writings he did not specifically name it. He described its painful effects by calling it a thorn. It was more than a briar or a thistle as we would surmise. The thorns of the east were long stout spines that were capable of penetrating a thick leather boot. Suffice it to say it was something that made him recoil in pain. It hurt him severely. He did refer to it as an "infirmity of the flesh" (Galatians 4:13) and it was the same affliction mentioned in II Corinthians 12:7. The inference is that the people in the churches where he had ministered knew what it was. If the Spirit of God had intended for us to know specifically it would have been clearly stated on the pages of the Scriptures.

It is a waste of time to speculate as to the nature of that thorn. That is a minor part of the experience and of little consequence. One might as well make conjecture as to the species of the lily to which Christ alluded, the nationality of the prodigal son or the color of the hair on the head of the rich young ruler. If we knew the particular infirmity we would be prone to think the lessons were for such a trial only. Because we know he suffered from a piercing thorn we can well suppose that his thorn was like ours. Thus we can profit from his experience. The important factor is not what the thorn was but why it was sent.

When this thorn stabbed his flesh what did Paul do? He did not deny its existence, whine in self-pity nor become bitter because of the experience. He did what you and I can and should do. He prayed. So severe was the trial that, like Jesus in Gethsemane, he prayed three times. His experience was further like that which is often ours in that no answer was immediately forthcoming. Nothing came from heaven but the echo of his own petition, as if to veritably haunt him. When you have a problem pray about it, repeat your prayer and still there is no answer what do you do? What should you do?

After such an experience Paul came to the sudden realization that the goading of the thorn was for a purpose. It was allowed by God to come his way. Instead of being only "a messenger of Satan" it became an auxiliary to God's purpose in his life. That thorn had a ministry for him. Eventually he realized a part of that purpose and twice he wrote, "lest I should be exalted above measure." A basic purpose of the thorn was to produce humility. When Paul accepted the thorn as being for good in his life the victory over it had just begun.

Once I visited a large mental hospital. When being shown the reception room where all patients enter the hospital, I remarked, "I imagine you have some protests in this room. Don't some of the patients avow that they are all right and rebel against being committed?"

"Some?" asked the attendant. "They all protest to a degree and we expect that." After a pause he spoke further. "When the patient realizes that something is wrong and that we are trying to help him, then he is on the way to recovery."

Although the analogy may seem strange, the lesson is plain. When we realize the thorn is for a purpose and stop threshing around, then we, like Paul, have taken the first step toward victory over it. Instead of something evil it is a tool in God's hand for good. The barb may still be present but it has lost something of its power to prick.

Paul had a problem. He prayed about it and his prayer was not answered. The thorn remained and gouged just as deeply as before. But now he sang and rejoiced. What brought about the change? The circumstances had not been altered. God had not intervened miraculously. It was Paul himself who had changed and that was accomplished through

a change of attitude. When he recognized that sufficient
grace was as much God's answer as the removal of the
thorn, then he had the victory. As long as he fretted and
demanded the thorn must go, he chafed under the experience.
When the spiritual insight came to him that God was working
a purpose in his life, then the song began.

Your thorn, like Paul's, can lose its piercing power when
your attitude changes. Fret, stew, question, complain and
thresh around and you will be miserable indeed. Instead,
let God's truth seep through. Rather than an emissary of
Satan, see it as a molding tool in the hand of the great
potter. Instead of being harmful, view it as a messenger of
good. Instead of a pestiferous nuisance accept its ministry
for your spiritual welfare. You may not change circumstances.
You may not change God's plan. However, you can change
your attitude and bring triumph out of apparent chaos. That
ability actually lies within your hands.

The oft-quoted verse of Ella Wheeler Wilcox is a vivid
illustration of this truth.

> "One ship drives east and another drives west
> With the self same winds that blow;
> 'Tis the set of the sails and not the gales
> Which determines the way they go."

The winds will blow and you have no human power to
stop them. If God does not choose to make them subside you
have but one alternative remaining. So set your sail that
those winds will guide you to the place of triumph rather
than to the rocks of despair. An additional verse says,

> "Like the winds of the sea are the ways of fate
> As we journey along through life,
> 'Tis the set of the soul that determines one's goal,
> And not the calm or the strife."

You set the sail and thus chart your course. You hold
the rudder which we call attitude. By your attitude toward
the thorn in the flesh you determine whether it shall mean
misery or joy, the mournful groanings of a sufferer or the

victorious shout of one who has triumphed over all circumstances.

Whether the thorn of your life is removed or remains,
rests in the hands of God. Whether it is a blessing or a curse
depends upon you and your attitude toward it. Will you
not join Paul in saying, "Most gladly therefore will I rather
glory in my infirmities, that the power of Christ may rest
upon me."

18

Marks of Maturity

"That we henceforth be no more children, tossed to and fro . . . but . . . may grow up in him." — Ephesians 4:14-15

The entire program of God points toward bringing His people into the full stature of Christ. We are born again and grow spiritually as any human being does, physically. We strive, or at least should do so, toward the utmost as fully-developed Christians. The task of preachers and teachers is not merely to get souls saved, but "that we may present every man perfect in Jesus Christ" (Colossians 1:28).

In this portion of Ephesians the apostle Paul sounds a call for Christian maturity. He exhorts us to "grow up" in Christ. We are admonished to cease being children and become adults. God put in the church apostles, prophets, evangelists, pastors and teachers "For the perfecting of the saints . . . for the edifying of the body of Christ" (Ephesians 4:12). Such ministry gifts are to serve "till we all come in the unity of the faith, and of the knowledge of the Son of God, unto a perfect man, unto the measure of the stature of the fulness of Christ" (Ephesians 4:13).

The above text presents the negative aspect in order to set for the truth more graphically. We are to cease being children and to become full-grown men. A modern version of the Bible expresses it in picturesque fashion. "No longer children, tossed by the waves and whirled about by every fresh gust of teaching, dupes of crafty rogues and their deceitful schemes."

Maturity is an attitude that enables a person to handle any situation as an adult. It is a state of having reached full development. Whether or not we are mature can be determined by certain abilities that we possess. The lack of them would indicate immaturity and childishness.

There are five marks of such maturity that are good tests in determining the stage of our spiritual development. They can be applied equally to our natural lives or our spiritual make-up.

1. *The ability to make independent decisions.*

The husband who cannot pick out his own neckties, but leans on his wife, is immature to a degree. The married woman who must consult her mother in even minor decisions has never grown up. He who leans on others as to whether to go to church, respond to an altar call, or to guide him in some spiritual action, is living beneath his actual age.

A mature Christian has a mind and convictions of his own. He will not be swayed by a crowd or by his friends, or by a dominant personality, when a principle or conviction is involved. He will be developed enough spiritually so as to be able to make the best decision for himself.

2. *The ability to assume responsibility for your own acts.*

My little son Kim accidentally spilled his milk at the table. When reprimanded by his mother he said, "Donnie made a face at me and made me spill it." He was still a mere child and rather weakly tried to blame someone else for what he had done.

Weak and childish individuals always find someone to blame whether it is logical or not. That habit started at the beginning of time. When reprimanded by God for his sin, Adam said, "The woman whom thou gavest to be with

me, she gave me of the tree and I did eat" (Genesis 3:12).
Then Eve found someone else to blame. "The serpent be-
guiled me and I did eat" (Genesis 3:13). Aaron made a
golden calf but when rebuked by Moses he blamed the
people. He said of the gold, "I cast it into the fire, and
there came out this calf" (Exodus 32:24). He tried to pretend
that the golden calf just happened, while the record says
that he, "fashioned it with a graving tool" (Exodus 32:4).

The mature person will accept responsibility for what he
has done, whether good or bad. He who is immature will
blame the hypocrites, the church, the pastor, his friends,
or anyone but himself.

3. The ability to give rather than receive.

Children are basically selfish and must be taught other-
wise. It takes a long training process to make them share
with brothers, sisters, and playmates. Some who have grown
physically and passed their majority are still children in
this respect. He who must always receive and never gives
is, at the best, very immature. Even his prayers are self-
centered. Like the prodigal son he continually says, "Give
me," instead of "Make me."

Giving or receiving temporal goods is only a small part
of this attitude. A major area touches on praise or credit.
A weakling thrives on praise but will never praise anyone
else. He is sensitive when people do not give him credit,
but he will never ascribe credit to anyone else. When his
program is a success his attitude is "glory be to me," but
if it fails he finds a scapegoat upon which to lay the
blame.

One of the keenest barometers of maturity or its counterpart is whether one gives or receives credit and praise.

4. The ability to distinguish fact from fancy.

Children can speak of Santa Claus and Jesus Christ in
the same breath. They cannot differentiate between the
real and the unreal. They hear both Christmas stories and
do not realize which is historical fact and which is myth.

The immature Christian rather gullibly accepts anything he hears. If it comes in a sincere tone of voice or in the name of religion it must be good. If it is a new or different thought, doctrine, or method, he never questions but wants to be one of the first to embrace it. Is it any wonder so many are whirled around by every fresh gust of teaching?

It is said of the Antichrist that he will deceive the very elect. At first glance that appears impossible but in observing the immaturity of so many professed Christians we can understand why it will happen.

The mature Christian, like the Bereans, searches the Scriptures daily to determine what is fact and what is fancy.

5. *The ability to adapt to new situations.*

Adaptability is a noble trait. Situations change in life. The immature person allows those changes to throw him and to upset his equilibrium. He who is full grown spiritually accepts them as a challenge.

The weak Christian who moves to a new community finds the differences insurmountable. None of the churches he visits is like the one back home. The people are friendly but there aren't the old familiar faces that he has known for years. The change is too much for such a hothouse plant.

A mature Christian faces such changes realistically. Outward circumstances are minor. His sustaining strength is drawn from the Lord and not from his surroundings. He adapts to a new situation by leaning more heavily upon the Saviour.

The admonition of the apostle Paul and the Holy Spirit is that we "grow up." Developing and maturing is not an overnight act. It is something that comes through a gradual process. Unlike physical growth, it is a goal toward which we strive and make consistent efforts.

On one occasion the apostle Paul wrote, "When I was a child . . . I understood as a child, I thought as a child: but when I became a man, I put away childish things" (I Corinthians 13:11). He had developed into an adult physically, mentally, emotionally, and spiritually. He was a mature Christian.

Have you, too, put away childish traits and become an adult Christian?

19

Pickets at the Pearly Portals

"Ye entered not in yourselves, and them that were entering in ye hindered." — Luke 11:52

Men wearing sandwich boards sauntered slowly at the entrance of a large industrial plant. For weeks they had been pacing that sidewalk like caged lions. The signs they wore told of a grievance against their employers. Once they had worked for the firm, but now they refused to do so. Not only did they choose not to enter the establishment, but stood on guard to make sure no one else did. Theirs was a selfish lot. They chose not to work and made certain that no one else would either.

Very few industrial firms have not heard the shuffle of picket's feet. Even the White House has been picketed by one group or another that had a protest to voice. Astounding though it may seem, there have even been pickets at the gate of heaven. Men were doing it in the day of our Lord and have done so in every succeeding generation, including the one in which we live. Jesus boldly confronted some such individuals and said, "Ye enter not in yourselves, and them that were entering in ye hindered."

During the earthly ministry of our Saviour, He was in

constant conflict with the scribes and Pharisees. They were His sworn enemies and used every means of chicanery and underhanded dealing to discredit him in the eyes of the people. They used deception, intimidation, slander, derision, and even boycotted Him. Knowing what was in the heart of man, Jesus recognized their hypocrisy and boldly faced them with it. He accused them of magnifying tradition over Divine commandments, self-justification, prayers and rituals for observations, proselytizing, and having only an exterior of piety instead of inward righteousness. He did not mince words but, in picturesque language, called them hypocrites, whited sepulchers, a generation of vipers, and then said they were of their father, the devil. It is understandable that His blunt words did nothing to lessen their hatred for Him.

It is disconcerting to be called a hypocrite. It is most humiliating to hear a public declaration that you are not on the way to Heaven — particularly if you are a religious leader. Whether or not you are inwardly aware of that fact, you do not want to hear it sounded from the housetops. Jesus' indictment of the Pharisees and scribes was most serious. It was decidely so in that he intimated that they deliberately chose not to enter Heaven's gate. They were not misled, duped or hoodwinked by some unscrupulous leader. They were the bell sheep and were leading the flock. In spite of their piety, culture, rituals, education and leadership, they were outside the gate and in a lost condition.

The other phase of Christ's charge was the most serious that could be laid at anyone's door. Of all the rebukes Jesus gave, this was the most calamitous. He indicted them with deliberate obstructiveness. Again the inference is that it was not accidental. With full knowledge of right and wrong, with an understanding of spiritual things, and with a consciousness of what they were doing, they had been barricading Heaven's portals to those who would enter.

When a man rejects Jesus Christ and suffers eternal death, it is a horrifying experience. What could be worse than to be lost? What more terrifying fate could a man suffer than

to be everlastingly locked out of Heaven? Casual consideration says there is nothing worse. And yet there is something
more appalling! It is to have missed Heaven and to know
that you have been responsible for the same thing happening
to hundreds of other souls. What a frightful fate has befallen
those of past generations who, with dulcet tones, have called
the throngs into "a way that seemeth right" but ended in
utter destruction. Out of financial advantage, intellectual
pride, human popularity, and other influencing factors has
come a leadership that has damned rather than blessed.
Could such individuals relive their lives, what a change
there would be! Were it possible for them to speak to this
generation, what a penetrating warning would sound forth
to errant leaders.

The leaders of Israel claimed exclusive authority to inter-
pret the Scriptures, and yet they silenced them by their
traditions. They possessed the key to eternal life, and yet
they locked the door and threw away the key. The love
of prestige, pomp and ceremony led them to choose those
things to the loss of God's blessing to themselves and others.
Like pickets at the pearly gate of Heaven, they "entered
not in [themselves], and them that were entering in [they]
hindered."

Why did Jesus speak these scathing rebukes to the scribes
and Pharisees? Certainly He did not enjoy such things and
had no delight in seeing them cringe. No one delights in
speaking blunt, harsh words. The average person would
rather avoid such utterances, and surely Jesus was no exception to that. Yet He repeatedly voiced such charges. Why?

The words of Jesus were not only a rebuke to the erring
but were also warnings. These religious leaders were outside
Heaven's gate, but as yet it was not permanent. They were
obstructionists and were hindering the salvation of others,
but there was still a possibility of a change. Had the final
die been cast, the words of Jesus would have been useless.
While there was life, there was still hope for them. Perhaps
sharp words would prod their consciences. Maybe rough
utterances would shake them to their senses and bring about

a turn toward the salvation of themselves and hundreds of others.

Whether any of them changed their ways we do not know. Whether they did or did not has been settled long ago. No more concern need be expressed for the hypocritical leaders of the first century. In the 20th century, however, there are still those who are deliberate stumbling blocks to thousands who follow in their steps. Like the picket, they refuse to go in, and yet they officiously deter those who in sincerity want to go God's way.

The words of Jesus still rebuke such a person; but more than that, they warn him. The mercy of God is still extended to that one, but it will not always be. The way to God is still open to him and to those who will happily follow his example. If you are that person, turn to enter that beautiful gate and, like Paul, say to those behind you, "Follow me as I follow Christ."

20

The Haunting Lament

"As thy servant was busy here and there, he was gone."
— I Kings 20:40

Many a sinner has lost his soul through his own neglect, but some are lost because of the neglect of Christians. A barbed reminder of such a possibility is given in the climactic sentence of a minor Old Testament parable.

In the midst of battle an officer entrusted a prisoner to one of his soldiers. When the time came for a report on his stewardship the soldier made a candid confession by saying, "As thy servant was busy here and there, he was gone."

The chief responsibility of the soldier was to look after the prisoner of war. Those were the orders of his superior and that task should have superseded all others. He lost a multiplicity of minor things. He was zealously busy about many legitimate tasks but through it all he lost the one who was entrusted to his care.

As we journey through life God charges certain individuals to our keeping. Whether or not these persons are aware of our official orders, we should be. When our lives run parallel to another, for a long or brief span, it happens in the providence of God so that we can influence that life and be a saving force.

1. *The charge to parents.*

In a more specific way than any other, God makes parents responsible for the lives and souls of their offspring. They have an obligation to provide not only for physical and intellectual needs, but for the spiritual as well. Nature demands that they take care of the first two but the latter can be easily neglected.

A sadder sound is seldom heard than the plaintive cry of a parent who has been "busy here and there" and suddenly his son or daughter is gone. The years sped by so rapidly. The formative period is in the past and the golden door of opportunity has closed. That father still has a child but he lives at a distance and is far removed from the God of his parents. A heart yearns to tell him of spiritual things but there is not the opportunity there was when the lad bounced on his knee. That parent prepared the child for life but not for eternity.

During the Klondike gold rush of 1898 the quick-fortune fever was at a high pitch. Not only men, but even women and couples rushed northward after the yellow god of the materialists. One adventuresome couple even took their ten-year-old son along and exposed him to the rough, vulgar crowds in the boom towns of the tundra.

Before a year was out that boy was killed in a needless and senseless accident. With sobered hearts the parents returned to civilization. As they walked down the gangplank in Seattle old friends called out, "Did you get any gold?" A heavy hearted father answered, "Yes, but we lost our son."

What shall it profit parents if they gain the whole world and lose their own children?

Oh, that we could fully realize how brief is the time we have with our children. At best we are together very little. They are really ours to influence for God far fewer years than they spend in the old homestead. Some have slipped from both us and God even before they leave to set up homes of their own. Then the parents must lament, "I was busy . . . and they were gone." Some children are lost because of their own neglect but others perish because of the early neglect of their parents.

2. *The charge to teachers.*

Every Sunday school teacher is weighted with a heavy responsibility for the souls of his pupils. His time to influence each life is far more limited than that of the parent. Hence he must make those fleeting weeks and months count. He may teach the same class for years but the pupils come and go through growth and promotion.

The work of a teacher is more than thoroughly studying a lesson, making an interesting presentation, keeping discipline or doing a necessary job. Teaching the lesson is not an end in itself but a means toward the conversion of the pupil and establishing him in the way of God.

The teacher who used the class session to give me interesting biographical sketches about leaders in art, science and music and other related fields missed a valuable opportunity to mold my life in its formative years. He did nothing to contribute to my soul's salvation. He was busy with minor matters and soon I was gone from his influence. That I am saved today is only through God's grace and the faithfulness of others.

Another teacher who misuses valuable time is the one who is trapped into talking about interesting, but valueless subjects. The alert minds of youngsters often conjure up questions that lead far from Scriptural truth and the teacher steps into the snare and follows them afield. Nothing harmful is said but valuable time is lost wandering "here and there."

The brief months and years have gone. The boy has grown to a manhood that is anything but glorifying to God, His Sunday school teacher, like the soldier in the parable, excuses himself by saying, "As thy servant was busy here and there, he was gone."

3. *The charge to neighbors.*

Even the person who is neither a parent nor a Sunday school teacher should be aware of his responsibility to those with whom he daily associates. Perhaps we do not influence fellow adults as much as children but still there are words to speak and examples to set. Did you ever consider yourself as a missionary to your place of employment? It may be amidst surroundings of blasphemy, smutty stories and vile conversation, but God has put you there to be a witness where it is badly needed. He has sent you forth as "sheep among wolves." For months and years you have greeted a fellow commuter, worked next to someone in a factory, waited on a certain customer or talked to a neighbor over the back-yard fence. You have conversed about incidentals but said little about the things of God. Perhaps you plan to do so some day and have assumed that your association will go on forever. Such contacts break much quicker than family ties or church friendships. Suddenly that man will not be on the bus each morning, the neighbor may move away or the obituary column may carry the news of the passing of the one to whom you had planned to bear witness. Suddenly the door of opportunity is closed. You frittered too long and now there remains only remorseful regret. While you puttered with minor matters a soul has gone beyond your reach.

One of the major assets of life is the ability to determine what things are important and to emphasize them. Just being busy is not enough. Anyone can keep active but it takes a discerning individual to budget his tasks and make his energies count.

The soldier in the parable was busy in a frenzied, desultory activity. He was doing many things and no one could accuse him of being idle. He did everything but his duty. While involved in nonessential tasks he failed in his major assignment and the person who was entrusted to his care slipped from his grasp.

The haunting lament out of the past should goad us to concern for the present and the future.

"I was busy . . . and he was gone."